Opening Lines

Approaches to the Scholarship of Teaching and Learning

Pat Hutchings, Editor
The Carnegie Foundation for the Advancement of Teaching

A PUBLICATION OF
THE CARNEGIE FOUNDATION
FOR THE ADVANCEMENT OF TEACHING

ACKNOWLEDGMENTS

Funding for this book and CD-ROM is provided by The Carnegie Foundation for the Advancement of Teaching and The Pew Charitable Trusts, which also jointly fund the program on which these materials are based, the Carnegie Academy for the Scholarship of Teaching and Learning (CASTL).

This volume features reports by eight Carnegie Scholars working with CASTL to develop a scholarship of teaching and learning that will advance the profession of teaching and improve student learning. As indicated in their reports, their work depends heavily on the support and interest of the larger group of Carnegie Scholars, as well as of colleagues on their campuses and in their scholarly and professional fields. CASTL's three components, described in the Preface, speak to the need for involvement on all of these levels. This volume reflects that involvement and could not have been produced without it. In turn, we hope the information here will deepen and extend that involvement.

Many members of the Carnegie staff—too many to name—contributed to the substance and production of this publication, reading and responding to drafts, consulting about design, and sharing ideas about the scholarship of teaching and learning. Thanks to all.

Book design by Leap O Faith Design. Photographs by Susan Vogel, Larry Sleznikow, Tom Cherry, Norton Photography, and Max Ramirez Photography.

Library of Congress Cataloging-in-Publication Data

Opening lines : approaches to the scholarship of teaching and learning /
Pat Hutchings, editor.
    p. cm.
Includes bibliographical references.
  ISBN 0-931050-68-5 (alk. paper)
 1. College teaching—United States—Case studies. 2. College
teachers—United States—Case studies.   3. Learning—Case studies.
I. Hutchings, Pat.   II. Carnegie Foundation for the Advancement of Teaching.

  LB2331 .O58 2000
  378.1'25'0973—dc21

                00-011249

For more information about The Carnegie Foundation for the Advancement of Teaching, please consult our Web site: **www.carnegiefoundation.org**.

Additional copies of this publication are available from:

Carnegie Publications
The Carnegie Foundation for the Advancement of Teaching
555 Middlefield Road
Menlo Park, California 94025
Phone 650/566-5128
Fax 650/326-0279

Single copies are $15. For information on bulk orders, contact Carnegie Publications.

CONTENTS

As THIS VOLUME GOES TO PRESS, the Carnegie Academy for the Scholarship of Teaching and Learning (CASTL) approaches its third birthday. Officially launched at the American Association for Higher Education's Conference on Faculty Roles and Rewards in January 1998, CASTL was at that time a blueprint for action that had barely begun, still much more a vision than a reality. It was a vision shaped by important past work, most notably the 1990 report *Scholarship Reconsidered* by former Carnegie Foundation President Ernest Boyer, and its 1997 follow-up, *Scholarship Assessed*, by Charles Glassick, Mary Taylor Huber, and Gene Maeroff. AAHE's own work on peer collaboration and review of teaching was an important foundation as well, as were developments in student assessment, classroom research, and a host of other initiatives on teaching and learning.

CASTL is now a centerpiece of the Carnegie Foundation's work, with three interrelated components. **The Pew National Fellowship Program for Carnegie Scholars** brings together outstanding faculty to investigate issues in the teaching and learning of their fields in ways that contribute to thought and practice. **The Teaching Academy Campus Program,** coordinated by Carnegie's partner, the American Association for Higher Education (AAHE), works with campuses of all types to build cultures in which the scholarship of teaching and learning can grow and flourish. Meanwhile, CASTL's **work with scholarly and professional societies** supports the development of new language, standards, vehicles, and occasions for conducting and exchanging the scholarship of teaching and learning.

As directors of CASTL, we are hardly unbiased observers of its work, but even our high hopes did not prepare us for the reception this three-fold program has met, or for the level of activity it has generated. Eighty-three Carnegie Scholars, in three cohorts, are developing and sharing examples of the scholarship of teaching and learning that enrich our sense of what is possible; indeed, the one frustration of the program is not being able to accommodate the increasingly rich pool of applicants. At the campus level, we confess to amazement. Within weeks of announcing the program, Barbara Cambridge, our wonderful and energetic collaborator at AAHE, was swamped with interest from campuses that saw CASTL as congruent with their own agendas and, indeed, as just the sort of external validation and impetus needed to move their work along. So great was the first flood of interest that we altered an original plan to start small and build (we imagined 80 campuses as a kind of ceiling). Today, over 170—from the University of Michigan to Middlesex Community College—are officially registered and at work. You can read their progress reports through the AAHE WebCenter, online at http://aahe.ital.utexas.edu. Their work is in turn bolstered by cooperation with twenty or so scholarly and professional societies, about half of which have shaped action proposals funded by CASTL.

A clear lesson of activity thus far is the growing interest in learning from and about the scholarship of teaching and learning. It is that interest this volume attempts to meet. In particular, it is intended for those who are intrigued with the idea of teaching as scholarly work but not quite sure how to put that idea into practice—faculty who have questions about their teaching and their students' learning but little training or experience in how to answer those questions. The eight Carnegie Scholars whose cases appear here are owed a debt of gratitude by those of us who can learn now from their experiences. Knowing these Scholars, we suspect they would want to thank (as we do) the larger group of Carnegie Scholars for providing a context and community in which work could unfold. Thanks also to The Pew Charitable Trusts, our major funding partner, and to the many folks on campuses, in the scholarly societies, at AAHE, and here at Carnegie who speed this work on its fascinating way.

Lee S. Shulman, President
Pat Hutchings, Senior Scholar
The Carnegie Foundation for
the Advancement of Teaching

Approaching the Scholarship of Teaching and Learning

Pat Hutchings
Senior Scholar, The Carnegie Foundation
for the Advancement of Teaching

T HE CASES THAT CONSTITUTE THIS VOLUME represent work in progress by faculty selected as Carnegie Scholars with the Carnegie Academy for the Scholarship of Teaching and Learning (CASTL). Each of the eight authors tells the story of her or his efforts at "opening lines" of inquiry into significant issues in the teaching and learning of the field. In particular, their accounts focus on the *doing* of this kind of investigative work—that is, on methods and approaches for undertaking the scholarship of teaching and learning.

A key principle of this volume is that there is no single best method or approach for conducting the scholarship of teaching and learning. Indeed, the cases illustrate a need for approaches that are useful and doable in the varied contexts represented by their authors. Mills Kelly, for instance, explores questions about teaching and learning at a large public research university; Donna Duffy undertakes her investigation in the quite different setting of a community college. Both public and private institutions are represented; several are urban, one is Catholic, and another, Spelman, is an historically black college for women. The authors' fields are diverse as well, including humanities, social sciences, natural sciences, business, and an interdisciplinary program. Several of the eight are senior faculty, well along in their academic careers; one is not yet tenured. All of these differences play into the way the authors think about and undertake their scholarship of teaching and learning. The desire to illustrate a variety of approaches, and to preserve the contexts and particulars of their use, underlies our decision to build this volume around cases. Cases capture details and differences.

But readers will find common themes as well. The cases were developed through a process designed to reveal aspects of the scholarship of teaching and learning that crosscut contexts and fields. This process began with two-hour phone interviews, conducted by me with each of the authors. The interview was turned into a rough transcript, which the author then reworked around a set of common topics or questions that emerged as the interviews were undertaken, and which appear as more or less standard headings in the finished cases collected here. For instance, all of the authors describe the process of formulating their question or questions. Each also describes the investigative strategies he or she considered using, how choices were made among these, how the various approaches worked or didn't, and what was learned from doing the work. In a final section of each case, the author offers advice to faculty newly undertaking the scholarship of teaching and learning. Our hope is that by organizing the cases around a set of standard elements we have made it easier for readers to extract transferable lessons and themes they can apply in their own work.

As a further aid to this task, an accompanying CD-ROM provides additional information and resources. For instance, Dennis Jacobs talks, in his case, about a focus group protocol he adapted and used as part of his study of at-risk students in chemistry; that protocol appears in the "analytical tools" section of the CD-ROM, where it can be accessed, adapted, and used by readers. Additionally, the CD offers samples of student work, artifacts such as syllabi and exams, and links to electronic course portfolios as well as leads to further resources relevant to "how to" questions.

The "opening lines" of the volume's title point to the process of undertaking inquiry. The phrase has another meaning, as well. The work reported in this volume is (or was at the time of writing) work that is at its *opening*, if you will, rather than its *closing* stage. Each case includes a section on emerging conclusions, but these are typically preliminary (though the CD-ROM includes more information of this kind for some of the cases, and all of the authors are writing and speaking about their work in other forums as findings emerge more firmly). The purpose here, in this volume, is to feature work at a fairly early stage—early in the particular investigation reported but also, for many of the authors, early in the experience of a scholar who is a relative newcomer to this kind of work and therefore learning from the process as it unfolds. As will be clear, many of the authors are actively thinking about where this work will take them next and how—or whether—it might find a more central place in their career trajectory.

This book represents "opening" work, too, in the larger sense that the scholarship of teaching and learning is not yet fully defined or conceptualized, making this an important time to examine emerging practices. We are lucky to have practitioners willing to go public at this stage so that the field can learn from their successes as well as from the challenges they face.

What can be learned from the case authors' work? Because the impetus for this volume is the need expressed by growing numbers of faculty for concrete, practical guidance about designing and conducting the scholarship of teaching and learning, the authors have provided a good deal of concrete, practical detail—about how to use a focus group, for instance, or ways to work with colleagues as co-investigators. In contrast, the purpose of this introduction is not to compile their suggestions but to set forward several larger themes reflected in the eight cases—themes that help build the conceptual and theoretical foundations needed for the practice of the scholarship of teaching and learning.

An Ethic of Inquiry

The opening section of each case focuses on the genesis and shaping of the question or questions the scholar wishes to examine. Indeed, this opening section is one of the longest in many of the cases, which speaks both to the difficulty of this first stage of work *and* to its usefulness as a window into the character of the scholarship of teaching and learning. How does it emerge as a practice? Why would an already too-busy faculty member want to do it?

Based on the cases, one answer is that the scholarship of teaching and learning often begins in quite pragmatic questions. Cindi Fukami explains the source of her question by telling the story of the wood cutter who never found the time to sharpen his saw and therefore wasted both time and energy. That, says Cindi, was the predicament in the MBA program at the University of Denver, where she and her colleagues had been employing a group-project assignment (a central element of a central course in the curriculum) that was clearly in need of "sharpening." The scholarship of teaching and learning provided the context to turn this sticking point into an opportunity for purposeful experimentation and study.

What's notable, however—in Cindi's case and others—is that the decision to examine an aspect of practice in a new way was not only a practical one but one with a deeper motivation as well. Continuing with an assignment that did not serve student learning had simply become untenable for Cindi; it didn't feel right. Similarly, for Dennis Jacobs the decision to examine the impact of an alternative section of General Chemistry began with his realization that students who could not succeed faced permanent roadblocks to next stages of their college work and career ambitions. "My empathy went to these students," he writes, "and I felt a responsibility to address what I saw as an injustice." Donna Duffy tells the story of wanting to find a better way to teach abnormal psychology to students who were already, in many ways, working against the odds. "Abnormal psychology is mostly about the *problems* that people face," she writes, "and to counter that I tried organizing the course around the more positive concept of resiliency. ... It's a more hopeful and hope-giving version of the course." As these and other cases in this volume illustrate, the shaping of a good question for the scholarship of teaching and learning is not only a practical and intellectual task but often a moral and ethical one as well.

Asking the right question can also mean a radical shift from usual practice. In an essay that has become a sort of seminal text for CASTL, Randy Bass, a faculty member in

American Studies at Georgetown University and a 1998 Carnegie Scholar, writes:

One telling measure of how differently teaching is regarded from traditional scholarship or research within the academy is what a difference it makes to have a "problem" in one versus the other. In scholarship and research, having a "problem" is at the heart of the investigative process; it is the compound of the generative questions around which all creative and productive activity revolves. But in one's teaching, a "problem" is something you don't want to have, and if you have one, you probably want to fix it. Asking a colleague about a problem in his or her research is an invitation; asking about a problem in one's teaching would probably seem like an accusation. Changing the status of the problem in teaching from terminal remediation to ongoing investigation is precisely what the movement for a scholarship of teaching is all about. How might we make the problematization of teaching a matter of regular communal discourse? How might we think of teaching practice, and the evidence of student learning, as problems to be investigated, analyzed, represented, and debated? (1, included on the CD-ROM)

The reports in this volume are cases of this process of posing problems, of making publicly problematic the important work of teaching and learning. They show us what it means to take seriously our professional responsibility as scholars to examine that work and to share what we discover and discern.

In the final "lessons learned" section of his case, Bill Cerbin puts it this way: "Like all forms of scholarship, the scholarship of teaching has to be motivated finally by personal commitments. ... The wrong reason to do the scholarship of teaching is because it's now listed in the criteria for promotion and tenure; that's a formula for turning important work into just a job, one more hurdle or task. I think there's an important message here about passions, and pursing ideas that really matter to you."

A Taxonomy of Questions

Every scholarly and professional field is defined in part by the questions it asks. It is useful, then, to examine the kinds of questions that characterize the scholarship of teaching and learning. The eight cases collected here help to elaborate a taxonomy of questions that has been emerging through the work of the Carnegie Academy for the Scholarship of Teaching and Learning (CASTL booklet, 5).

One kind of question is about "what works." Not surprisingly, this is where many faculty begin—seeking evidence about the relative effectiveness of different approaches. ("What works" questions in the scholarship of teaching and learning are cousins, it might be said, to the assessment movement—though for many faculty assessment comes with a hard "prove it" edge that is quite different from the "ethic of inquiry" adduced just above.) Mills Kelly, for instance, traces his scholarship of teaching to a question from his department chair, who asks whether students in Mills' Web-based history course are learning more than they would in traditional print-based versions of the course. This is, Mills realizes, a "wonderful question" that he himself has not asked, and he sets out to answer it. Dennis Jacobs, similarly, began his investigation with a desire to know more about the effectiveness of an alternative design for the general chemistry course at Notre Dame. Indeed, for both Mills and Dennis the power of the "what works" question lies, in part, in the fact that such questions are *shared*—by Mills' chair, and, in Dennis' situation, by colleagues who

want to know what works and how, therefore, to invest limited departmental resources. In short, the "what works" question is often one that has a ready audience, an element much to be wished for in this and other forms of scholarship, and one that is most usefully considered in the original framing of the question rather than as an afterthought.

A second kind of question focuses on "what is." Here the effort is aimed not so much at proving (or disproving) the effectiveness of a particular approach or intervention but at describing *what it looks like*, what its constituent features might be. Investigations of this descriptive type might, for instance, look at the dynamics of class discussion around a difficult topic; they might be efforts to document the varieties of prior knowledge and understanding students bring to a particular topic or aspect of the discipline. Among the eight cases collected here, Sherry Linkon's is perhaps the clearest illustration of the "what is" type. Her aim, as she tells us, is to understand interdisciplinary courses from the students' point of view—an antidote to the usual focus on the experience of the teacher. "People [in my field] have published a lot of teaching stories—wherein the teacher tells about what she taught, how she taught, what happened, and how the students liked it. These are wonderful stories, but they don't necessarily get us to a deeper understanding of what's going on for students." Sherry thus sets out to describe and systematically analyze the student experience of interdisciplinary courses in her program at Youngstown State. This topic is being explored by several other Carnegie Scholars as well, and Sherry sees as a next step in her work collaboration and data sharing through which their respective findings can be tested and refined across settings.

The "what is" question is closely related to a third type, which Lee Shulman calls "visions of the possible." Mona Phillips' work exemplifies this category. She begins with a question about how her sociology students understand and engage in the process of theorizing (as opposed to their knowledge of particular theories) but, as she describes in the initial section of her case, she becomes increasingly focused on fostering "an emotional dimension of learning," which she speaks of as joy. "I want to understand more about how I can help students see themselves as part of the wonderful process of understanding the world around them and their position in it." To create (and examine) a course with this kind of goal—a goal, as she notes, that many sociologists would not endorse or embrace—is indeed to commit to and enact a vision of the possible. It recalls Bill Cerbin's point, quoted above, about the origin of this work in personal passions.

Mariolina Salvatori, too, illustrates the kind of inquiry that begins with a vision of the possible. In her case the context is an English classroom in which students' "moments of difficulty" are seen and treated not as shortcomings or deficits (the student does not understand the final couplet of the poem because she's just not smart enough) but as opportunities for learning. Indeed, Mariolina sees such moments as windows, often, into defining elements and issues in the particular text or even the larger content of the discipline; that is, difficulties can be used to uncover what is most essential to understanding.

But Mariolina's work also illustrates a fourth type of question, which is not so much exploring an aspect of practice as it is formulating a new conceptual framework for shaping thought about practice. This type of question is, thus far in the scholarship of teaching and learning "movement," underrepresented. That's too bad because—as is illustrated by Mariolina's collaboration with colleagues (Mills Kelly is one of them) who are adapting her framework to other disci-

plines—new models and conceptual frameworks generate new questions that can, in turn, enrich the scholarship of teaching and learning and extend its boundaries.

Bill Cerbin agrees. Noting that faculty interested in problem-based learning (the topic of his study) may find clues to practice in what he has done, he nevertheless anticipates that the greater contribution, in the long run, may lie in "some useful theoretical distinctions both to the concept of learning with understanding and also to teaching for understanding. A global idea that comes out of this investigation is how important it is to understand why some things are hard for students to learn." This kind of theory building, Bill argues, is an important element of the scholarship of teaching and learning.

It is important to note that these four types of questions are by no means mutually exclusive. As noted, Mariolina's work spans at least two of the categories. Dennis Jacobs started with a "what works" question but later added a more process-focused dimension to his investigation, looking not only at impact and effectiveness but (using videotapes of student cooperative-learning groups as well as focus groups) at understanding more deeply *what is* happening in the course. Sherry Linkon begins with a "what is" question about her students' experience of interdisciplinary teaching and learning but she soon finds herself "doing a lot of playing around" with questions (perhaps this is a fifth type) about methods of inquiry, noting, "I saw this as a chance not only to learn more about interdisciplinary studies but also to explore methods for understanding more about the student learning process. Part of my goal is to experiment with different approaches, to see whether I like them, to see what I get from them."

Finally, it should be noted that the taxonomy of questions described here is only one model. Craig Nelson, a biologist from Indiana

University and a 2000 Carnegie Scholar, recently developed a document (included on the CD-ROM) of "selected examples of several of the different genres of the scholarship of teaching and learning," which he defines in large part by unit of analysis: reports on particular classes, reflections on many years of teaching experience, and summaries and analyses of sets of prior studies. Craig entitles his document "How Could I Do the Scholarship of Teaching and Learning?" and his title speaks to the value of such efforts at classification, part of which is to put forward possibilities and encourage practice of different types. Additionally, this kind of mapping of the field may be helpful in showing how various instances of the scholarship of teaching and learning connect, where the lines of relationship lie, where there are gaps that need to be filled.

Thinking about Methods

A central focus of this volume is, of course, methods. And a central lesson about methods leaps immediately out of the details: that a mix of methods will tell you more than a single approach. Looking *across* the eight cases we see a rich array of possibilities for gathering and analyzing evidence: course portfolios, the collection and systematic analysis of student work (often by secondary readers, sometimes with newly developed rubrics), videotape, focus groups, ethnographic interviews, classroom observation, large-scale longitudinal tracking, questionnaires, surveys, and more. And *within* each individual case we see the variety of ways these approaches can be combined in order to give the fullest possible picture.

On the one hand this methodological pluralism (within and among projects) is common sense. Teaching and learning are complex processes, and no single source or type of evidence can provide a sufficient window into the questions we most want to explore. Indeed, as Craig Nelson points out, "Learning and teaching are complex activities where approximate, suggestive knowledge can be very helpful, and, indeed, may often be the only kind that is practical or possible." But faculty new to this work are likely to begin with a more limited set of methodological possibilities, recognizing the need for a larger and more varied set only as the investigation unfolds. For many such faculty, this means becoming familiar with approaches that are totally new and even against the grain, a process (as the case authors make clear) that can be both exciting and intimidating.

What is also clear is the power of the disciplinary context in shaping the way faculty think about and design their approaches to the scholarship of teaching and learning. Mary Huber, a senior scholar at the Carnegie Foundation, has been exploring disciplinary styles as part of her work with CASTL, and her paper on the topic has prompted vigorous discussion among Carnegie Scholars and other faculty interested in the scholarship of teaching and learning. The cases here further illustrate many of her points.

Mills Kelly, for instance, talks about methods in what is essentially a homecoming story. Early in his work, he tells us, he found himself casting about, trying to figure out how to do this thing called, somewhat dauntingly, "the scholarship of teaching and learning." Behaving like a good historian, he went to the library and began reading about the use of multimedia in the teaching and learning of his field; what he found was a body of educational research (mostly *not* focused on history or, indeed, on any particular discipline) employing "a methodology that I knew nothing about—a new language, a use of control groups, a scientific approach." It was not familiar or comfortable ground: "I'm not an educational researcher by training. I'm an historian."

It was only later, when Mills read the work of another historian who had been studying the teaching and learning of history, that he realized the relevance of his own background—that the tools and dispositions of an historian might, that is, stand him in good stead in addressing questions about teaching and learning. His question about recursive reading, for instance, is an historian's question about a process that Mills sees as essential to the doing of history. And his electronic course portfolio can be seen as a kind of *chronicle* of the course, an account of its unfolding over time, with links to relevant artifacts and evidence.

The influence of the discipline on the conduct of the scholarship of teaching and learning is illustrated nicely by Sherry Linkon's case, as well. Noting the need to ask her questions about the student experience of interdisciplinarity "at various levels and in various contexts," she says, "This is very like my process in doing my regular research. I look at different sources and look for patterns of meaning, relationships, and so forth. Sometimes I feel like I'm not getting anywhere because I'm not finding clear answers. Other times I feel like I'm learning a lot despite the fact that I'm not finding clear answers. I'm a humanities scholar, after all. How often do I find really definitive answers on anything?"

Clearly the methods of the scholarship of teaching and learning are shaped by the methods of the disciplines; beginning with those methods is a right idea not only because they are familiar but because they're warranted by scholarly peers who might build on the work. At the same time, one sees in these cases a good deal of methodological borrowing and influence, across fields. Cindi Fukami finds a helpful model in Donna Duffy's use of an external observer in the classroom as a way to give objectivity. Focus groups, a method developed in marketing circles, are employed by Dennis Jacobs, a chemist. Mariolina Salvatori's project design is reshaped by challenges posed by two sociologists who ask questions her colleagues in English probably would not. These cases document the power of methodological conversation and collaboration *across* fields, as faculty borrow approaches and perspectives from colleagues in other areas. Developing a broader, more sophisticated repertoire of methods is clearly one of the challenges facing this work, and a necessary step in advancing the scholarship of teaching and learning as a field.

Common Ground

To examine the questions and methods of the scholarship of teaching and learning is to raise an issue about its relationship to the larger universe of educational research. Generalizing about the difference is difficult, it turns out, because "educational research" encompasses a considerable variety of approaches. See, for example, Lee Shulman's opening chapter in the second edition of *Complementary Methods for Research in Education* where he describes a wide range of work along five dimensions: problems, investigators, methods, settings, and purposes. As he points out, many of the approaches in evidence today could not have been foreseen a decade ago. Moreover, many of the methods he describes overlap with those described in this volume as examples of the scholarship of teaching and learning. It is useful, nevertheless, to identify the features that characterize the scholarship of teaching and learning. What do the eight cases tell us in this regard?

First, the scholarship of teaching and learning is deeply embedded in the discipline; its questions arise from the character of the field and what it means to know it deeply. Thus, Mona Phillips describes her investigation as follows: "I'm trying to describe as fully as I can a new way of thinking of my field and what it means to teach in keeping with that transformed view." Similarly, when Donna Duffy redesigns an abnormal psychology course around the concept of resilience, she is working out of a concept in her field, redefining an aspect of its teaching and learning. When Mills Kelly asks about students' habits of recursive reading he is asking an historian's question. Mariolina Salvatori's interest in moments of difficulty reflects, she tells us, the field's (and her own) theoretical conception of reading and interpretation.

Second, the scholarship of teaching and learning is an aspect of practice. In contrast to research done by a "third party" examining the practice of others, this is work, if you will, "in the first person," undertaken by faculty looking at their own practice (and sometimes the practice of colleagues with whom they teach or share curricular responsibility). Indeed, for some of the case authors, the scholarship of teaching is hard to distinguish from teaching itself. It's not just *about* one's teaching; it is an element within teaching, hard to separate out. Mariolina Salvatori's "difficulty paper" is, for instance, a central element of her teaching rather than a special "intervention." Similarly, Mona Phillips' investigation relies on regular activities of the course, including student papers and the "ideas assignment." Mona talks, too, about how her investigation changes the role of students, making them more active agents in shaping and examining the processes of teaching and learning. Indeed, the involvement of students in the doing of the scholarship of teaching and learning—as co-investigators and agents, rather than as objects—is a theme that has arisen in CASTL's Campus Program (Cambridge). As Mona also points out, the work entails a kind of "going meta," a different way of looking at the activities in which she and her students engage as the course unfolds. Stephen Fishman and Lucille McCarthy (in a wonderful book-length account of their collaboration and development as scholars of

teaching) describe the challenge of a process that "requires faculty to disengage from their normal activities, change their usual professional gaze, and view their classrooms in a highly reflexive way" (27).

In this sense, the scholarship of teaching and learning entails a challenge that several of my Carnegie Foundation colleagues working with CASTL call "the moving target" and that Bill Cerbin speaks of as a "changing script." "In reality," Bill writes, "I was teaching this class *as* I was experimenting with it and studying it, and under those conditions you sometimes *have* to change the script as you go because your best judgment tells you that a change would be an improvement for the students." For some, this may imply that the scholarship of teaching and learning is less systematic or rigorous than other forms of scholarly work. In fact, Bill's account of having to "change the script as you go" is offered by way of explanation for not being able to conduct full-fledged "design experiments"—an approach he aspires to in subsequent stages of this ongoing work. But for Mona Phillips this need to "strike a balance between rigor and flexibility" and to let the investigation "unfold and take shape as the course itself, as well as the students' experience, unfolds and takes shape" is part of the power of the scholarship of teaching and learning.

Finally, the scholarship of teaching and learning is characterized by a transformational agenda. One of CASTL's publicly stated goals is to foster "significant long-lasting learning for all students" (CASTL booklet, 3), and the desire to create stronger curricula and more powerful pedagogies runs through all the cases in this volume. The scholarship of teaching and learning might then be defined as scholarship undertaken in the name of change, with one measure of its success being its impact on thought and practice.

What then is the difference between the scholarship of teaching and learning and other forms of educational inquiry? To what extent do the features described above characterize a distinctive field of investigation? My colleague Mary Huber recently shared with me an email message from a mathematician who asked the question this way: "What *exactly* is the difference between the kind of work being done by someone like Alan Schoenfeld [a faculty member at the University of California–Berkeley and recent president of the American Educational Research Association] and what Carnegie is promoting as the scholarship of teaching and learning?" Mary's response is, I believe, congruent with the characterization put forward above, but she makes a wider point as well, worth quoting in full:

I have always seen the scholarship of teaching and learning as a broad canopy, under which a wide range of work could thrive. This could include work of the kind Schoenfeld and his educational research colleagues do, the work most Carnegie Scholars are doing, but also the work that scholarly teachers are doing when they make inquiries into their classroom practice, document their work, and make it available to peers in relatively informal settings (the brown-bag lunch, for example). The innovation here is to invite regular faculty, and not only education specialists, to see this kind of inquiry as a regular aspect of their work as professors. For purposes of faculty evaluation, the most elaborate work (the Schoenfeld kind) might be presented as scholarship of discovery (i.e., research), and the least elaborate as a form of reflection on teaching and learning (i.e., teaching). Those working the middle range could go either way. And naturally, any one person might over a span of time engage in different ways.

As this introduction makes clear, we are increasingly able to characterize the scholarship of teaching and learning both in terms of concrete examples and more general, distinguishing features. As Mary's comment eloquently suggests, the point of doing so is not to choose camps but to find common ground; to bring the energy and intellect of more people, from various communities and traditions, to bear on important educational issues.

Indeed these communities (or rather, these types of work, since one person may do different things at different points) enrich one another. The scholarship of teaching and learning may open up new questions that, over time, prompt major new lines of educational research. Educational research may suggest models and strategies that can be explored in the scholarship of teaching and learning and in scholarly teaching practice. What CASTL aims to do is to foster forms of reflection and inquiry that can make the most of these opportunities and intersections.

In this spirit, it's important to conclude this introduction by noting that the eight Carnegie Scholars who have here generously opened their work to public view are part of a growing community of scholars. They draw on and acknowledge one another's work and the work of the much wider circle of faculty participating in CASTL. They both benefit from and contribute to changing conditions on campuses that can make the scholarship of teaching and learning (and its various cousins and relations, whatever they're labeled) more central and valued—an outcome supported as well by the efforts of scholarly and professional societies that have been working to give prominence to teaching. There is, in short, a larger and very lively ecology around the cases that follow here. In a closing chapter, Lee Shulman reflects on the longer-term prospects for that ecology. But first the cases …

REFERENCES AND RESOURCES

Bass, Randy. "The Scholarship of Teaching: What's the Problem?" *Inventio* 1.1 (1999). 18 August 2000 <http://www.doiiit.gmu.edu/Archives/feb98/randybass.htm>.

Cambridge, Barbara. "What Is the Scholarship of Teaching and Learning?" *AAHE Bulletin* 52.4 (1999): 7–10.

The Carnegie Academy for the Scholarship of Teaching and Learning. Informational program booklet. Menlo Park, CA: The Carnegie Foundation for the Advancement of Teaching, 1999.

Fishman, Stephen M., and Lucille McCarthy. *Unplayed Tapes: A Personal History of Collaborative Teacher Research*. Urbana, IL: National Council of Teachers of English, and New York: Teachers College Press, 2000.

Huber, Mary Taylor. "Disciplinary Styles in the Scholarship of Teaching: Reflections on the Carnegie Academy for the Scholarship of Teaching and Learning." *Improving Student Learning: Improving Student Learning through the Disciplines*. Ed. Chris Rust. Oxford: Oxford Brookes U. Center for Staff and Learning Development, 2000.

Nelson, Craig E. "How Could I Do the Scholarship of Teaching and Learning?" Unpublished paper, 2000.

Shulman, Lee S. "Disciplines of Inquiry in Education: A New Overview." *Complementary Methods for Research in Education*. 2nd ed. Ed. R. Jaeger. Washington, DC: American Educational Research Association, 1997. 3–30.

Investigating Student Learning in a Problem-Based Psychology Course

William Cerbin
Psychology, University of Wisconsin–La Crosse

Bill Cerbin

William Cerbin's graduate education was in the areas of developmental and educational psychology. He earned a PhD in educational psychology with an emphasis in language and cognition from the University of Chicago and a master's degree in learning and development from Columbia University. Since 1980 he has been a faculty member at the University of Wisconsin–La Crosse where he is professor of psychology and also assistant to the provost and vice chancellor for academic affairs. At UW–La Crosse, he has served as the university assessment coordinator and was the founding director of the Center for Effective Teaching and Learning. In addition, he has been co-director of a UW System program for junior faculty called the Wisconsin Teaching Fellows Program.

UW–La Crosse is a master's level institution that enrolls 9,300 students. Bill has taught a wide range of undergraduate and graduate courses in the areas of developmental and educational psychology, including language and cognitive development, psycholinguistics, an honors seminar, and the teaching apprenticeship for psychology; he has also directed numerous undergraduate research projects. Bill's research interests focus on learning with and teaching for understanding. He has given workshop presentations related to teaching and student learning at state, regional, and national conferences and on many college campuses. The interview for this case study took place in October 1999.

My project investigated the development of student understanding in an undergraduate educational psychology course. I redesigned an existing course and taught it with a problem-based learning format, focusing on two important factors related to student understanding. One is how students' prior knowledge and beliefs about the subject affect their understanding of new ideas, and the second is whether students are able to transfer, or think with, newly learned subject matter to solve novel problems. The results show that students could, in some cases, "think with" the subject matter, but in others they continued to rely on prior beliefs and non-disciplinary knowledge to solve problems.

Framing the Question

Some of my interests and the way I framed my questions are a result of my disciplinary background. As a psychologist, I study cognition, and I have a long-standing interest in the effects of prior knowledge on new learning, and in how knowledge transfers (or doesn't) to a new context.

But my questions also come out of my own practice as a teacher, dating back a decade or so, as I have become increasingly focused on my own students' learning—how it occurs, or doesn't, why students learn some things and not others. My interest in these questions led me to experiment with various teaching practices over the years. I also began looking for different ways to investigate more systematically what was going on in my own classroom, which is what led to the course portfolio I developed for my educational psychology course in 1992. In turn, the portfolio activity really focused my attention on what students were learning in my class—and on how problematic that learning was. As I documented and analyzed a number of activities in the class—activities that I saw as representative and that could therefore depict for portfolio readers what goes on in the class—I discovered that there was a continuing gap between what I expected and hoped students would learn and what they were actually producing for me.

One episode in particular prompted this realization. We had studied learning theory in class for several weeks, and I had every reason to believe from the students' written work and class discussions that they had a grasp of the major concepts. Then I had the class do an exercise in which they had to apply learning theory to explain a particular teaching strategy called "reciprocal teaching." This was a straightforward transfer problem—they had studied learning theory and this new problem asked them to use those concepts. But in this instance, they had a great deal of difficulty drawing on the concepts we were studying in the class. Their explanations had a "person on the street" quality that reflected little disciplinary knowledge. Students constructed their explanations from ideas they brought to the class with them, ideas that were part of their own personal models about what constitutes teaching and learning and had little to do with the concepts we had studied in the class.

Since developing the portfolio, I've continued to examine these kinds of episodes, with the result that my thinking about student understanding has gradually shifted from a simple if-they-say-it-and-it-sounds-good-I'll-believe-that-they-understand-something to a next phase in which I'm much more aware of the multifaceted nature of understanding. This shift has been an interesting experience for me. There was a time in my own teaching when I was pretty confident that when students produced a right answer (by which I mean they produced an answer that sounded like something that I had said or something that the book said), I was relatively satisfied and tended to believe that they also had some understanding behind that answer—that it wasn't just verbatim information, but that they had some deeper grasp of it. Then, gradually, that confidence began to unravel as I used more informal kinds of writing activities in which I was getting students to think on paper, in the moment, about particular concepts or ideas that we were talking about in class. These writing activities were ungraded, and they turned out to be a window into what students were thinking, and what lay behind their test answers. What I saw was a whole lot messier than what I had anticipated.

As I was starting to focus on problems of student understanding in my classes, there was an emerging literature in the cognitive sciences about students' misconceptions of important ideas in a variety of disciplinary areas. Research was starting to show that students' prior knowledge about a subject often includes misconceptions that influence how and whether they learn new ideas. That literature helped me interpret my students' performance in a new way. You could say that this research started to influence my own personal model of teaching and learning. Rather than attribute my students' poor understanding to their lack of ability or effort or to poor teaching on my part, I began to see learning with understanding as inherently problematic. Not very surprisingly, given my disciplinary background, my investigations into my students' learning were not so far afield from my other scholarly pursuits. This turned out to be an experience in which my classroom observations were remarkably consistent with the things I'd been reading about in the literature on conceptual change and development.

My investigation really is a culmination of a number of years of study, which I wanted now to focus more sharply on the factors that interfere with or impede the development of student understanding in a course like educational psychology. I subsequently became very interested in teaching for understanding, trying to develop more successful ways to advance student understanding of the subject matter. I decided to adopt a problem-based learning approach in the class. This, too, was a natural evolution for me since one of the most glaring problems in my class was students' difficulty in applying knowledge to new situations and problems.

The Context: A Course in Educational Psychology

My investigation takes place in the educational psychology course I've been teaching for almost twenty years, which means I've probably taught it at least fifty times. Over the years I've modified the course extensively, not just updating the subject matter but trying out different teaching strategies. But I decided to make a much more radical change this time as part of my scholarship of teaching project, transforming the course to a problem-based learning (PBL) format.

Of course problem-based learning has a long history in medical education, but it has been slower to catch on in other fields, including psychology. There is a kind of Old Testament version of PBL, which I spent some time studying in the literature. But the way I teach differs from the standard model. The long and short of it is that the course is built around problems instead of being built sequentially around a series of topics. The problems are complex, open-ended scenarios I have created in order to focus on domains of subject matter in the course. Certainly a problem can embed a whole host of sub-problems, and this is one of the challenges because students will uncover problems that aren't really the ones the instructor had in mind. He or she can't fully anticipate how the problems are going to "play," which is one of the things that makes this kind of teaching a challenge.

I've created seven or eight of these problems for the educational psychology course, and during the semester we move from one to the next. I have tried to establish multiple contexts that invite transfer of knowledge by using several problems drawing on the same subject matter. As a result, what students learn in one problem becomes relevant to one or more subsequent problems. This departs from a standard educational psychology course, which tends to survey a range of separate topics. I try to use a set of problems to accomplish greater depth of understanding.

As a consequence of these changes, the organization of the course differs completely from previous versions. In my pre-PBL life I would have known exactly where we were on any given day in the semester. I would have been very much in control of the information. What the transition to PBL has required me to do is to back off from controlling the situation and instead allow students to encounter these problems. Rather than always telling everything to students in advance, much of what I do now is respond to students' attempts to interpret and solve the problems.

Let me be clear about this. In the past, I was the tour guide for the subject matter, organizing and presenting important information to students. Now, problems come first. Students may do assigned reading and writing assignments in preparation for working on the problems, but much of what I do is in response to students' inquiry. For example, in the process of working through a problem students might overlook or misinterpret key material. In this case, I may intervene with a brief lecture or discussion to elaborate or clarify material immediately relevant to the problem situation. I do a good deal of just-in-time teaching.

> "What I'm after is a way to build students' understanding of the subject so that concepts become part of the way they analyze and interpret new situations."

In the big picture what I'm after is a way to build students' understanding of the subject so that concepts become part of the way they analyze and interpret new situations. In this class, I'm trying to influence the way students interpret, analyze, and respond to teaching and learning situations—their "pedagogical thinking." And that's a great leap. For the most part, students can think about course concepts. They read the assignments, write about important concepts, and discuss them in class. But it is a different matter to "think with" the concepts, to use them as a way to analyze and solve a problem.

My hope is that a course constructed and taught using problem-based learning—though not all by itself—begins to change students' sensibility and the way they look at a situation, that rather than making sense of things through whatever first impulse leaps to mind, they can learn to set that first reaction aside and try to figure out what framework would be most appropriate for explaining it. That's the transition I'd like to foster in my students—to be able to move from simple, "textbook" answers to an analysis of the deeper structure of the problem. It's their ability to make this leap that I'm trying to investigate.

Gathering the Evidence

This project does not fall neatly into a specific research design category. I wanted to examine how students' understanding of a subject develops throughout a semester in a problem-based learning environment. Basically, I used the problems I was giving to students in class as the focus for examining their learning with understanding. Each time they worked out a problem (which might take a week or even two), I collected their work—that was the evidence I was most interested in—and analyzed it in terms of the model of understanding I had developed, looking for evidence that such understanding was there or not there, and to what extent.

One of the interesting challenges was getting a handle on the concept of understanding. Fortunately, good minds have preceded me, and the work of several scholars has been very important. Grant Wiggins' work, for instance, has helped me to make abstract ideas about understanding very concrete; the framework he presents on this topic is very, very useful. I also relied on the teaching for understanding work from the Harvard Project on Teaching for Understanding, using especially Martha Stone Wiske's compilation *Teaching for Understanding: Linking Research with Practice* (Jossey-Bass, 1998). Recent work by John Bransford and Dan Schwartz at Vanderbilt has been extremely helpful as well.

I have focused extensively on the quality of students' explanations as an index of their understanding. For instance, one problem depicted a seventh grade science class in which children were doing quite poorly. My students had to analyze the scenario and figure out what could be done to improve the seventh graders' learning. Most importantly, they had to explain why their proposed "solutions" would actually work to advance the adolescents' science learning. I was less concerned about their strategies than about the quality of their explanations—whether they could develop a compelling rationale for their approach. Consequently, I might use a rubric like the following to evaluate their understanding:

Underdeveloped understanding	Developed understanding
Contains misunderstandings, clichés, unwarranted personal opinion	"Thinks with" the course concepts
Answers describe but do not explain	Explanations integrate course concepts
Weak integration of course concepts	Explanations supported by material from the course
Ideas are vague, nonspecific	Fully developed ideas
No examples to illustrate ideas	Relevant examples illustrate idea

My ability to examine students' movement toward more "developed understanding" depended on three critical steps: I had to know what I was looking for, set up situations that offered students the opportunity to learn, and try to analyze student work in order to get some sense of how they were progressing in the class. This may not sound like anything different from what all teachers do when they grade student work. But I was trying to focus on understanding—a multidimensional concept that is not easily quantified. For every written assignment, I gave students a rubric that delineated the criteria for evaluating their understanding and other features of their work (for instance, quality of formal writing). Other ways to monitor student understanding presented themselves, but I have not had time to implement them. For example, I videotaped class periods throughout the semester and would like to examine the quality of the discourse in the class in order to note how students talk about—and with—course concepts in discussions and presentations. I would be especially interested in whether and how discourse progresses or reflects more sophisticated use of ideas.

I should also say that I had at one time hoped that I would be able to do this work as a set of design experiments. A design experiment examines how and why a specific design for something works. In my case the design is a certain kind of learning environment intended to influence student understanding. I still hope to move to that kind of approach eventually. But if I hold the work that I've done thus far up to the criteria for design experiments, it's not there yet. It's there in intention, but I haven't had the stability in the learning environment that would allow me to claim the requisite degree of control. In reality I was teaching this class *as* I was experimenting with it and studying it, and under those conditions you sometimes *have* to change the script as you go because your best judgment tells you that a change would be an improvement for the students. But as a result, I didn't have control, in terms of introducing a certain kind of situation, controlling the variables, and then analyzing student performance.

> "In reality I was teaching this class *as* I was experimenting with it ... and under those conditions you sometimes *have* to change the script as you go because your best judgment tells you that a change would be an improvement for the students."

On the other hand, I look at what I've done as a first step toward setting up more full-fledged, formal design experiments. And the next step in that direction would be to build small-scale experiments I could do in the classroom, which I would not be able to do had I not done this kind of teaching. That is, I would never be able to create a very smart experiment about this kind of learning setting had I not done this kind of teaching. I just wouldn't have the insight into what goes on in the classroom, or the sense I now have of how students respond to it. I can imagine starting with the *theory* of problem-based learning and constructing experiments that are pretty ill conceived. But my experience with this class, though I cannot call it a design experiment, was nevertheless a crucial step, since it has given me a much richer sense of what could be of interest in a more full-fledged experiment.

Emergent Findings and Broader Significance

What's emerging from this work? This question makes me want to go back to something that I've heard Lee Shulman say, which also appeared in the recent *Change* piece by Pat Hutchings and Lee (1999), about "theory building" as an important component of the scholarship of teaching. Independent of the kind of empirical work entailed in my investigation, the theoretical work is really quite interesting. We need models of learning with understanding that not only have intellectual integrity but are accessible broadly to faculty across the disciplines. I hope that my work eventually can contribute some useful theoretical distinctions both to the concept of learning with understanding and also to teaching for understanding. A global idea that comes out of this investigation is how important it is to understand why some things are hard for students to learn. It is very difficult to teach for understanding effectively without having some grasp of how students are likely to interpret, explain, and apply the subject matter.

Let me explain this by contrasting two ways to use a lecture to promote understanding. One is the traditional method in which the instructor develops a well-organized, clearly told story with good examples, visual images, and other representations of the material to illustrate ideas. Behind this approach is the belief that a well-told story makes the subject matter more accessible to students, and if they "study" the story, students will arrive at the teacher's understanding of the subject. Of course we know that even when the lecture is brilliant and the explanations are crystal clear, students can walk away with very different understandings of the subject. That said, I do agree that a well-told story is more accessible than a poorly told one and would advocate telling only good ones!

An alternative approach to lecture is to use it as a response to students' learning—after they have developed some ideas about the subject or tried to figure out some of the concepts. Insight into students' knowledge, beliefs, and interpretations ought to influence what story to tell and how to tell it. What I am saying is an updated version of an idea espoused thirty years ago by educational psychologist David Ausubel who said, "If I had to reduce all of educational psychology to just one principle, I would say this: The most important single factor influencing learning is what the learner already knows. Ascertain this and teach him accordingly" (1968, epigraph). I am suggesting that what is important is not just what students know, but how they think with what they know. A teacher who is attuned to students' thinking will make different decisions about what to tell students and how to support the development of their understanding than a teacher who simply lectures according to a pre-planned and inalterable syllabus.

Another kind of conclusion relates to the *practice* of teaching. I'm thinking that some people won't care whether this study produces statistically significant results but instead they might be very interested in what it reveals and illuminates about teaching in this problem-based way. They might want to get some sense of what this kind of teaching is like, the *experience* of it, which they wouldn't be able to get just by reading theories of learning or problem-based learning.

Some of what I have learned in this project is not so much conclusions as it is deepened insights and convictions about some things I believed before but didn't understand clearly. For one thing, I now believe much more firmly that changing students' minds, moving them to "deep understanding," is quite a bit harder than is usually recognized. And if you already think it's hard, well, it's even harder than that. The other thing is that it's especially hard in a brief period of time; the fifteen-week semester is a fleeting moment in the development of ideas and it's pretty hard to expect great transformation in that time frame. That's not to say that some good things can't get started, but I'd really like to be able to look at the long-term development of student learning, across a number of years, as well as how it all fits together

> "I now believe much more firmly that changing students' minds, moving them to 'deep understanding,' is quite a bit harder than is usually recognized. And if you already think it's hard, well, it's even harder than that."

with teaching and curriculum. My questions would be about whether what happened in such-and-such a class influences the way students think in a next class or down the line somewhere, especially when they begin to encounter real conflicts and situations in the field versus things invented in the class.

Conditions for Doing the Scholarship of Teaching and Learning

Starting with a very practical point, one thing that made it possible to do this work was participation in the Carnegie program, because the program increased my motivation and encouraged me to get it done. That's important because it was a sizable leap to take. In this sense, being a Carnegie Scholar is like having a research grant; it provides that kind of encouragement. I don't think I could have done this work without the program. I would have wanted to, but probably I couldn't and wouldn't have.

I suppose another condition to be mentioned is financial resources. But frankly I don't think the financial needs are huge. Many campuses offer teaching improvement grants that might provide modest funding for someone to take on a project like this.

What really made a difference for me was not so much financial resources as having like-minded colleagues. On my own campus I've been working essentially alone. This may not be true for some of the other Carnegie Scholars. For me it was largely a function of being so deeply immersed in the work and so busy that I just couldn't find occasions to sit around and talk with others about it. The Carnegie Scholars program met this need. Even though we were all over the map, geographically, it helped to know that there were other people investigating similar questions. Being able to touch base with others, to float an idea on our listserv—even fairly modest connections like these pulled me along at times and kept me going. It was very helpful to feel a part of something larger. And I don't think that condition always exists on campuses, where professional development around teaching is often focused on assisting individuals and providing training in new teaching approaches, but less often on creating a community. I've had an interest for a while now in developing a faculty seminar that would create this kind of community—one that would do the things the Carnegie Scholars did—where people working on something are willing to sit down as scholars do in a research seminar, to talk and to have the benefit of feedback and advice and critique from colleagues.

Benefits of the Work

For me the scholarship of teaching has been a kind of professional lifesaver. I have found it quite difficult in my setting to sustain a basic research program while also teaching four courses and doing the requisite service work on campus. In particular, my early work on language development in fairly young children was quite divorced from what I was doing day to day in the classroom in a teaching-intensive campus setting. Although I could use tiny bits and pieces of that work in one course, it certainly wasn't a seamless experience. So that sense of disconnection, combined with the fact that it was logistically very, very difficult to continue my original research, literally forced me to look elsewhere for scholarly activity. And the good news was that my interests began gravitating toward understanding student learning. For a while I was studying informal reasoning processes in students in my own classes, and I did studies with freshmen enrolled in general psychology and those sorts of things, but I still had not made the transition to investigating my own practice in my own classroom or to seeing this as an arena for my scholarly interests. The course portfolio was the big move in that direction, and the investigation I'm reporting on here is an even more sustained example. I'm not sure what forms this work will take in the future—whether I can do more formal design experiments or whether it will continue to be more exploratory work. Nonetheless, for me the transition has been complete. I am fully invested in trying to contribute something to the understanding of college teaching and learning.

Lessons Learned

What I would say to others attempting this kind of work is this: Find something that you really care about, something you're really interested in learning about, something that fascinates you. Like all forms of scholarship, the scholarship of teaching has to be motivated, finally, by personal commitments. There have to be aspects of teaching and learning that pique your curiosity, and those are the things that you should go after in your investigations. The wrong reason to do the scholarship of teaching is because it's now listed in the criteria for promotion and tenure; that's a formula for turning important work into just a job, one more hurdle or task. I think there's an important message here about passion, and pursuing ideas that really matter to you.

REFERENCES AND RESOURCES

Of the following references, I've annotated those I found most helpful as starting points for theory, research, and practice related to teaching for and learning with understanding.

Ausubel, D. P. (1968). *Educational psychology: A cognitive view.* NY: Holt, Rinehart and Winston.

Bransford, J. D., and Schwartz, D. L. (in press). Rethinking transfer: A simple proposal with educational implications. In A. Iran-Nejad & P. D. Pearson (Eds.), *Review of Research in Education* (Vol. 24). Washington, DC: American Educational Research Association.

Bransford, J. D., Brown, A. L., & Cocking, R. R. (Eds.). (1999). *How people learn: Brain, mind, experience, and schooling.* Washington, DC: National Academy Press. This book-length report summarizes important developments in the science of learning. Accessible to a nonspecialist audience, the book examines such topics as differences between novices and experts, conditions that improve students' ability to apply knowledge to new circumstances and problems, the design of learning environments, teacher learning, and effective teaching in history, mathematics, and science. This volume provides teachers with a thorough grounding in contemporary theory and research, and highlights important implications for teaching.

Brown, A. L. (1992). Design experiments: Theoretical and methodological challenges in creating complex interventions in classroom settings. *The Journal of the Learning Sciences, 2* (2), 141–178.

Center for Problem-Based Learning (1998). What is the relationship between problem-based learning and other instructional approaches? <http://www.imsa.edu/team/cpbl/whatis/matrix/matrix2.html> (June 30, 2000). This site, which is part of the Center for PBL site at the Illinois Math and Science Academy, provides an extensive comparison of PBL to other types of teaching approaches. The center's URL is: <http://www.imsa.edu/team/cpbl/cpbl.html>.

Cerbin, Bill (2000). The development of student understanding in a problem-based educational psychology course. <http://kml.carnegiefoundation.org/gallery/bcerbin/index.html> (2000, July 3). This Web site documents work I have done with problem-based learning in my own classes.

Dewey, J. (1933). *How we think.* New York: D. C. Heath.

Gardner, H. (1991). *The unschooled mind: How children think and how schools should teach.* NY: Basic Books.

Hutchings, P., & Shulman, L. (1999). The scholarship of teaching: New elaborations, new developments. *Change, 31* (5), 11–15.

McTighe, J., & Wiggins, G. (1999). *The understanding by design handbook.* Alexandria, VA: Association for Supervision and Curriculum Development.

Perkins, D. N. (1998). What is understanding? In M. S. Wiske, *Teaching for understanding: Linking research to practice.* San Francisco: Jossey-Bass.

Problem-Based Learning and Assessment Research Centre (PROBLARC) (1999). Bibliography of the Australian problem-based learning network. <http://www.newcastle.edu.au/services/iesd/learndevelop/problarc/bibliography.html>. This site, part of the Problem-Based Learning and Assessment Research Centre (PROBLARC) site at the University of Newcastle, Australia, provides an extensive online bibliography of material about PBL. The center's URL is: <http://www.newcastle.edu.au/services/iesd/learndevelop/problarc/>.

Samford University (2000). Problem-based learning at Samford University. <http://lr.samford.edu/PBL/index.html> (2000, July 3). This site includes links to PBL resources around the world.

Schwartz, D. L., & Bransford, J. D. (1998). A time for telling. *Cognition and Instruction, 16* (4), 475–522.

Stone Wiske, Martha. (Ed.). (1998). *Teaching for understanding: Linking research with practice.* San Francisco: Jossey-Bass. This book is the product of a six-year collaborative research project by school teachers and researchers at the Harvard Graduate School of Education. Although it focuses on precollegiate teaching, it is applicable to university-level teaching as well. According to the teaching for understanding (TfU) model, there are four fundamental elements in teaching for understanding—generative topics that afford possibilities for deep understanding in a subject, goals that explicitly state what students are expected to understand, performances of understanding through which students develop and demonstrate understanding, and ongoing assessment. The book provides interesting examples of these elements from actual classrooms and examples of student performance. This volume should be valuable for any instructor who views better student understanding as a primary goal of teaching.

University of Delaware (2000). University of Delaware problem-based learning. <http://www.udel.edu/pbl/> (2000, July 3). This site provides links to PBL resources around the world.

Wiggins, G. (1998). *Educative assessment: Designing assessments to inform and improve student performance.* San Francisco: Jossey-Bass. This book, a precursor to *Understanding by design* by the same author, challenges common assessment practices and offers a comprehensive approach to the design and practice of assessment intended to improve student performance. The book examines authentic assessment, the nature of feedback, how to use assessment to promote understanding, how to assess understanding, and how to design assessments and create assessment systems.

Wiggins, G., and McTighe, J. (1998). *Understanding by design*. Alexandria, VA: Association for Supervision and Curriculum Development. This book proposes that understanding is revealed to the extent that one can explain, interpret, apply, empathize, and have perspective and self-knowledge. The authors describe a process by which teachers can design experiences and materials to be consistent with these facets of understanding. A key component of the process is a way to assess understanding. Toward this end, they offer a rubric that defines different "levels" of understanding and suggest ways to evaluate them. This is a valuable book for those who want to translate abstract notions of understanding into concrete, observable aspects of student performance.

Wiggins, G., & McTighe, J. (1998). *Understanding by design Web site.* <http://ubd.ascd.org/index.html>.

Williams, S. M., & Hmelo, C. E. (1998). Learning through problem solving. *Journal of the Learning Sciences, 7* (3&4).

Wiske, M. S. (1998). *Teaching for understanding: Linking research to practice.* San Francisco: Jossey-Bass.

Resilient Students, Resilient Communities

Donna Killian Duffy
Psychology, Middlesex Community College

Donna Killian Duffy

Donna Killian Duffy is professor of psychology and co-coordinator of the Activating Learning in the Classroom (ALC) program at Middlesex Community College, Bedford and Lowell, Massachusetts. She earned her PhD in psychology in 1976 at Washington University. She is co-author, with Janet Wright Jones, of *Teaching Within the Rhythms of the Semester*, and co-editor, with Robert Bringle, of *With Service in Mind*, a monograph on service learning and psychology, published in 1998 by the American Association for Higher Education.

In 1991, Donna received an International Award for Teaching Excellence presented by the International Conference on Teaching Excellence at Austin, Texas. Since 1995 she has worked on two grants from the Campus Compact National Center for Community Colleges, "The Faculty Role: From the Margin to the Mainstream" and "2 + 4 = Service on Common Ground." The focus of the grants is to expand and strengthen service-learning initiatives in community colleges across the nation. Donna received the Thomas Ehrlich Faculty Award for Service Learning in 1999 for her work in connecting service in the community to student learning in classrooms. The interview for this case study took place in February 2000.

Using resilience as a theme I ask the students in my abnormal psychology course to complete either service-learning projects in the community or more traditional assignments. Throughout the semester, they collaborate in teams to analyze the authentic dilemmas that grow out of these assignments, using multiple perspectives. Team members integrate course material, propose specific solutions, and identify community resources that support resilience. With this exchange of information, reinforced and informed by my written impressions of the class, assignments crafted specifically to assess student understanding of resilience, and classroom observations performed by an anthropologist-colleague, I am trying to foster a dynamic learning environment that results in deep, long-lasting learning.

Framing the Question

Several issues and questions weave through my inquiry. The first is the dilemma of getting students in an abnormal psychology course to appreciate the complexity and the human aspects of the problems they read about in their textbooks. This dilemma, in turn, prompted me to begin using service learning, in other words, trying to provide students with a better sense of the realities behind what they were reading by asking them to learn in community settings. This strategy brought with it another issue, which is that it's not feasible to require the service-learning component for all my students; some have this "real-world" learning experience and some do not. So I'm interested in how I can get the learning from different settings to complement each other, making differences among students' learning a source of strength and further learning.

Another strand of issues involves the fact that students in the course are easily overwhelmed by the problems they read about, or see in the community, or experience in their own lives. Abnormal psychology is mostly about the *problems* that people face, and to counter that I tried organizing the course around the more positive concept of resiliency. I'm now teaching this version of the course for the third time. It's a more hopeful and hope-giving version of the course, and it engages students effectively in the course content. For example, an older student hesitant to join the class stated that she changed her mind immediately when the topic of resilience was introduced. She said, "It was a sense of moving right to the goal [that] made me want to stay in class and learn more."

Another issue—and this is an issue in the field of psychology in general—is public policy. Many of the topics we study in abnormal psychology have policy implications, but in most courses those implications are never addressed. I aimed to change this. The focus on resilience starts to generate questions students wouldn't have posed otherwise. Students begin to ask, "Why aren't we doing more to develop resilience in our communities and ourselves? What works best?" As students address these questions they begin to develop what Altman (1996) calls "socially responsive knowledge," an understanding of social issues in communities and the experience and skills to act on social problems.

Finally, all of these issues are shaped by my own work in the community, as a therapist dealing with problems in the schools and with people. I'm very aware of the difference between the textbook presentation of disorders and the actual experience of individuals with disorders in the community. The need to bring students to deeper, more authentic forms of understanding—as we discussed a good deal in the Carnegie Scholars Program—is something I'm strongly committed to. I see students go out to work in the community and they say, "Gee, I didn't really understand this when we read about it in class; it's much different, not at all what I expected." For example, a student commented that the "textbook presents disorders in organized categories but when I deal with people in the community, it's much more confusing. People belong in many categories and a lot of them overlap." In class students learn labels for things (a client has generalized anxiety disorder or bipolar disorder), but those of us who work in community settings know that the labels are not always useful because there are multiple ways of describing things, and labels are shorthand for a much more complicated reality. In my final Carnegie essay, "Swamps and Scholarship," I traced a student's struggles with explaining complicated realities; these struggles provide a window into the student's understanding of course material as it unfolded over the semester.

Behind all of these issues is a central dilemma I'm grappling with—which is that when teachers expose students to authentic learning they also lose control. And that makes assessment much more difficult. My scholarship of teaching project is an attempt to understand more about what this process of authentic learning entails.

The Context: A Course in Abnormal Psychology

The foundation for my scholarship of teaching project was the redesign of my abnormal psychology course. As I mentioned, a central element in this redesign was the introduction of resiliency as an organizing theme and a new lens for students to view the field. I began experimenting with this idea several semesters ago and have made refinements since then in an attempt to integrate the theme a little more tightly into some of the rest of the subject matter. These changes have resulted in a new course guide.

I've also introduced a three-part critical incident group project. Students work in teams of two or three throughout the semester. A student working in the community describes a critical incident from a service-learning site, other students relate the incident to material from the course, and then all students reflect on new understanding as a result of the process. The critical incident examples have been complex and multifaceted (for example, a seven-year-old with behavioral problems who had already been in five foster homes, a seventh grader reading at a second-grade level, and a middle-aged man with schizophrenia who did not take his medication). Students recorded their discussions and then worked to create a final paper. The majority of students were able to link the incident to course material effectively; the explanations of "new understanding" showed more variation and depth among student groups than they had in past classes with students working individually. For example, students working at community sites often make assumptions about an experience based on the facial expressions and vocal tones of people involved. In the group project, partners challenge these assumptions, using a more critical analysis to work toward alternative explanations. Out of their community work, these students would in turn present authentic problems to classroom partners, motivating them to find workable solutions. The classroom partners often used articles or Internet sites to suggest a solution to a specific community dilemma. This exchange of information into and out of the classroom created a dynamic learning environment that required all students to consider multiple perspectives while reflecting on course material. Because groups discussed the critical incident project throughout the semester, they were able to work through ideas gradually, to test out theories, and to appreciate that most complex human problems do not have easy answers.

I've also added a new form of assessment this semester, based largely on the discussions Carnegie Scholars have had about teaching for understanding, and what constitutes "deep" understanding. For the students who are not working in a community setting, I designed a final project that asks them to create a program that will engender resilience on a particular problem in some identified age group. For example, some of the students are interested in creating a drop-out prevention program for middle-school children. How would they go about doing that? It just happens that some of the other students who *are* working in the community are working in such a program. It is called GEAR UP (Gaining Early Awareness and Readiness for Undergraduate Programs) and is funded by the United States Department of Education. My hope is that the first group (not in the community setting) will visit the GEAR UP group, exchange ideas, and build a conceptual scaffolding on which they can walk back and forth and exchange ideas. In asking students to design something, I hope to prompt "performances of understanding," as defined by Perkins (1998), that is, activities that go beyond the rote and the routine, and always involving something of a stretch.

Gathering the Evidence

The course, as you see, has several new elements, and my project entails seeing how those elements work, how they play out, what happens. For instance, I am interested in moments like the one that occurred just recently in class. We were having a discussion about attention deficit disorder and one of the students began to explain the topic in terms of the concept of resiliency. That's the kind of connection I'm very interested in. I want to somehow track those moments, which means paying closer attention. I have been recording impressions after each class in a journal, raising questions and reflecting on ways to link concepts throughout the course. These journal entries have helped me to learn more about the gradual ways in which students connect or fail to connect ideas.

> "We were having a discussion about attention deficit disorder and one of the students began to explain the topic in terms of the concept of resiliency. That's the kind of connection I'm very interested in."

One of my efforts in this regard was accomplished through collaboration with a colleague, Susan Thomson, a cultural anthropologist, who visited my class as an observer, bringing along techniques from her field for coming into a new culture and seeking to understand it. She and I are writing about this collaboration, which I think has potential in the scholarship of teaching.

I also used a survey to find out more about my students: how much work their jobs require, how many courses they take, and what other kinds of commitments they hold. The answers are pretty discouraging because the majority are working thirty or forty hours, and are single parents or have other serious commitments on their time. On top of all this they're taking multiple courses.

I had used a version of the survey in earlier semesters but as part of my Carnegie work I created a more detailed version. Following some of the Carnegie Scholars' discussions about student understanding, I felt a need to get a better picture of the diversity, and the conditions, of learners. If students can't put in the time, they won't reach deep understanding. Our Carnegie Teaching Academy group at Middlesex Community College had a similar conversation: We as faculty may create "perfect" materials, but if the students don't devote enough time, their learning will be limited.

This presents an assessment dilemma in which faculty are continually frustrated by students' unrealistic appraisal of how much time course work requires.

To learn more about this, and to help students learn about themselves, I gave each student a sheet to map out their use of time for the twenty-four hours of each day over a full week. I explained the task in terms of the need to create a context for success in the course. I was pretty tough about this, pointing out to students that if their life left little time for study, they would be better off dropping the course than staying and failing. And a good number did leave. I'm sure that was not such positive news from the registrar's point of view, but from mine it's the right thing. Students set themselves up for failure, and then they fail, and then they feel badly about themselves. And this keeps happening. I'm sure I'll still have some in the class who will have this problem, but I see my approach as one step toward helping to build resiliency in my own students. The focus on resiliency as a course theme allows me to talk to them about this quite directly, which I do from the beginning of the semester.

Emergent Findings and Broader Significance

One thing that came up through the collaboration with my colleague in anthropology is that for a lot of students in a community college setting there's a lack of fit between what they will verbalize and what they will write. Maybe this is true of all students, but it's particularly marked in community colleges. It's one of the things my colleague identified through her observations and work with my students, and it's a very interesting problem for assessment. These students often have good ideas, but their motivation to write about them is not high because they've not been successful as writers. So the question is how to celebrate their good ideas and then move them to write about those ideas.

A few years ago I saw a clear example of this issue while assessing the final projects of two students who had worked at the local horseback-riding program for individuals with disabilities in our community. One student wrote a well-organized paper but received mediocre-to-poor evaluations from the supervisor at the site, with comments such as "does not relate to individuals," "difficult to work with," and "has a negative attitude toward clients." Another student wrote a marginal paper yet received stunning comments from the supervisor, including "incredible in connecting to clients," "anticipates potential problems in the setting," and "would hire him tomorrow." If I had not included the supervisor's comments in assessing the project I would never have obtained an accurate picture of what went on. Still, the question is how best to incorporate all aspects of work in arriving at a final grade.

Which brings me back to what I have learned about my students. In a class of twenty-eight, for instance, several are recovering from addiction, many have learning disabilities, four or five are single parents, some are immigrants, and, as I said earlier, most of them are working thirty to forty hours a week. They're needy on a lot of levels. But what's also true is that the community college learning experience can transform the lives of these students. When I talk to other community college faculty,

I hear stories about this, about making a real difference. Mark Katz (1997) in his book *On Playing a Poor Hand Well* presents the concepts of turning points and second-chance opportunities. The community college often creates a second-chance opportunity for students who have had negative experiences of education.

My point is that this circumstance, this vision of education, makes assessment a delicate task. I have to be fair in measuring levels of understanding but I also have to recognize the tremendous variety of circumstances represented in the class, shaping assessment to support and foster transformation rather than snuffing it out. Often, community college students have had debilitating experiences with teachers who did not value them. They haven't fit the model. We need to extend the range of what we value by opening up assessment to different forms of intelligence, different ways of knowing. Of course it's important for students to become proficient writers, but we have such a focus on the written word that we can't appreciate that people can know something in other ways. Wlodkowski and Ginsberg (1995) state that the basic purpose of assessment should be to engender competence. My goal is to create a diverse set of measures that will provide complete and fair assessment while also building competence as students progress through the different phases of the semester.

I should also mention a quite different kind of result from this work—one I couldn't have anticipated—which is that I'm now working with local sixth-grade classes through the GEAR UP project described earlier. Because the topic of resilience fits in well with the goals of the project, I am developing—together with other participants—ways to include resilience in activities at the schools. I'm also collaborating with a high school class through the American Psychological Association's Psychology Partnerships Project. Both of these opportunities have evolved from my work this past year, and I'm excited about how this idea of resiliency has begun to take hold in other contexts.

Conditions for Doing the Scholarship of Teaching and Learning

My colleagues in the Carnegie Scholars Program have provided much support. Indeed, our discussions shaped many of the things I'm doing. The dilemma of sharing what we do is that everyone is busy doing his or her own project. We need to develop more mentoring relationships that can support and sustain ideas over time.

On my own campus, it was a bit easier. Talking about teaching is positive and collaborative. No one suggested that I was wasting my time. Our dilemma at Middlesex has more to do with figuring out what we mean by scholarship, and where the scholarship of teaching fits at an institution that values teaching highly but does not have many of the habits and traditions of scholarly exchange and peer review.

The other thing that was very helpful to me is a sense among those of us working on the scholarship of teaching that we're trailblazers, that we're creating new genres, new forms of inquiry. We need to be comfortable exploring alternative paths and also with the realization that some of those paths may not work out—an easy comment to make but less easy to deal with when things really don't work. Working with like-minded colleagues means having an oasis—a refuge in which to regroup and refocus as the journey progresses.

Benefits of the Work

What is the value of this work? I was at a meeting with people I work with in a clinical setting. Someone was talking about a seven-year-old with many problems and how "he was just never going to make it." And I was thinking if we don't start to address this, then this is the seven-year-old we're going to see moving through the educational system and through our lives. What drives me in all my work is my sense that we just have to find ways to keep from writing people off, giving up on them. And my hope for the scholarship of teaching is that it will help open up our appreciation for the variety of learners and the need to make the most of many different kinds of talents.

> "My hope for the scholarship of teaching is that it will help open up our appreciation for the variety of learners and the need to make the most of many different kinds of talents."

I think of a recent essay by Alexander Astin (1998, 22) about underprepared students and about the absolutely crucial mission of higher education in helping these students succeed—and what the world will be like if we fail in this. He states that the problem in higher education is that "we value *being* smart much more than we do *developing* smartness." So my view of the scholarship of teaching is a long-term transformative one. I hope not just to do some discrete project but to change the way we think about educating diverse learners and developing "smartness."

Lessons Learned

One of the most useful frameworks for the scholarship of teaching and learning is the chapter by Lee Shulman (1998) on course anatomy in the AAHE volume *The Course Portfolio*. It sets out a framework within which scholars of teaching can work. In a workshop I recently did with several other Carnegie Scholars, we used that five-part framework of vision, design, enactment, outcomes, and analysis as a way of thinking not only about a course but also about a project in the scholarship of teaching.

Something else I have found useful in helping people get started is to ask them to talk about an experience from their teaching that had been particularly positive or challenging, and then to highlight some part of that. In the workshop, I gave them marking pens to do the highlighting literally. This activity makes the point that when you're doing the scholarship of teaching, you're highlighting an experience and then looking at it more closely. People seem to like this image. It puts the emphasis on something immediate and concrete; it starts with what they are already doing. This is important for most faculty because we are all so crunched for time. It's critical to start small and to set time limits for the inquiry. Initially I wanted to change too many things at once—this was unrealistic and overwhelming. The process worked better when I focused only on the "highlighted" parts of my course and established realistic time limits for completing the work. It was helpful to keep reminding myself that investigating learning, like learning itself, is a gradual process that unfolds over time.

I think that community college faculty are often very innovative but we need help in presenting our innovations to a larger academic community. The good news is that there are lots of currents moving in this direction. Community colleges have long faced the student diversity that many four-year institutions have begun to encounter only recently. In the Carnegie Teaching Academy on our campus we have spent considerable time trying to deal with the issues resulting from this diversity and have been studying ways to create learning environments that will engender more intrinsic motivation in students. Our initial attempts at translating theory into practice have been mixed, but it is encouraging to have groups of faculty discussing ways to improve learning in a particularly challenging environment.

REFERENCES AND RESOURCES

Altman, I. (1996). Higher education and psychology in the millennium. *American Psychologist, 51* (4), 371–378.

Astin, A. (1998). Higher education and civic responsibility. *National Society for Experiential Education Quarterly*, Winter, 18–26.

Katz, M. (1997). *On playing a poor hand well.* New York: W. W. Norton.

Perkins, D. (1992). *Smart schools: From training memories to educating minds.* New York: Free Press.

Shulman, Lee. (1998). Course anatomy: The Dissection and analysis of knowledge through teaching. In P. Hutchings (Ed.), *The course portfolio: How faculty can examine their teaching to advance practice and improve student learning* (pp. 5–12). Washington, DC: American Association for Higher Education.

Wlodkowski, R. J., and Ginsberg, M. B. (1995). *Diversity and motivation.* San Francisco: Jossey-Bass.

Looking Through a Different Lens: Inquiry into a Team-Taught Course

Cynthia V. Fukami
Management, University of Denver

Cynthia Fukami

Cynthia V. Fukami is professor of management at the University of Denver Daniels College of Business. She earned her PhD in organizational behavior at Northwestern University. Cindi reports that the acts of recognizing, enhancing, and contributing to the scholarship of teaching have constituted a fundamental theme in her career as a professor. She has addressed the scholarship of teaching through several avenues. She has been very active in a professional association for teaching, the Organizational Behavior Teaching Society, and has helped to bring the scholarship of teaching to the forefront in her major disciplinary professional organization, the Academy of Management. Currently, she is associate editor of the *Journal of Management Education*. At the University of Denver, she has actively participated in her college's efforts to embrace a multidimensional model of scholarship. Additionally, she has published several scholarly works and given many presentations at national conferences on teaching. The interview for this case study took place in March 2000.

Based on the literature on collaborative learning, and the literature on effective teamwork, my colleagues and I re-engineered the team project assignment in High Performance Management, an interdisciplinary team-taught course in our MBA core. At the end of the quarter, students completed questionnaires containing two measures: perceived team effectiveness and roles played in the team project. Analysis of the data, from both students and faculty, indicated that the new team project resulted in increased team effectiveness. The teaching team using the re-engineered project reported that they had received some of the best work they had ever seen from our students for this assignment. The assignment is now being used in all sections of this course with continuing positive results.

Framing the Question

The best way to explain the impetus for my project is a story that Carnegie Scholar Sally Foster Wallace tells about the woodcutter: His saw was so dull it doubled the time to cut the wood, and made the work much harder, as well. Finally, after many months of this situation, the woodcutter exclaims, "If only I had time, I'd sharpen that saw." That was my case exactly. My colleagues and I had been teaching the High Performance Management course for about five years, and one of its main themes was teamwork; we gave reading assignments about teams, we had students work in teams, we did team building through an Outdoor Leadership weekend, and we required team projects. And every time we taught the course, the team project was a fiasco. The more we tried to fix it, the more broken it became—more broken, more complicated, more of a problem. This was particularly frustrating because teamwork is something our field of organizational behavior and management is supposed to be expert at.

My question for the scholarship of teaching arose, therefore, when I began saying to myself, if only I had some time I'd really try to fix this problem. And then almost by magic, the Carnegie program was launched. When I was invited to be part of it, I knew instantly what I'd do: make a better team project for the course.

The Context: A Team-Taught Course on Teamwork

When I originally envisioned this project, I assumed I would conduct it in my own classroom. But as the quarter approached, I began to have concerns about that arrangement, for several reasons. First, all of my investigations into teaching and learning up to that time had taken the form of what I would call the reflective essay—a report on something I had done in my own class, and my evaluation of how well it had worked. I collected no systematic data, and did nothing to try to capture voices or perspectives other than my own. Essentially, I was dispensing sage advice about what to do in the classroom. So it felt like an important step for me in my own professional development to try to do something more systematic, more rigorous, more impersonal and detached from my own experience.

I also hesitated to try the project in my own classroom because I worried about introducing bias. The students evaluate me, as well as my team-teaching colleague, at the end of the quarter, and I evaluate them by giving grades. This seemed to me a built-in bias, that I might be too invested in the course's success to evaluate it objectively. So I thought of an alternative, which was to wait until the next quarter when I would not be teaching the course in question, and then enlist my colleagues as collaborators. I would work with them to design a new team project, and then investigate the impact of that new design in their sections of the course rather than my own.

Meanwhile, I realized that I needed a conceptual framework to structure my project. With this need in mind, I spent some of my summer residency at Carnegie exploring the relevant literature. Two sources proved particularly useful: the work by David and Roger Johnson on cooperative learning in higher education, and the work by Elizabeth Cohen on teamwork from the K–5 context. From these sources I developed a conceptual framework for examining teams in the classroom. This framework also drew on an article from the management literature, which students read for the course, by Jon R. Katzenbach and Douglas K. Smith, called "The Discipline of Teams."

The next step was to sit down with my two colleagues who would be teaching the sections I was going to study and negotiate what shape the team project would take. I made suggestions, they responded, and we ultimately arrived at a compromise project design. It was important that they be comfortable with the final design decisions. My contribution involved bringing research-based principles of collaborative learning into our thinking; my colleagues provided the wonderful insight that the team project should be *about* teamwork. In other words the new focus of the redesigned team project was teamwork itself.

The good news in this arrangement was that I felt I had the kind of distance I needed to adequately study the effects of this change. The bad news was that I couldn't do everything I wanted to do. I could only go as far as my colleagues were comfortable going, and I had to worry about meeting their needs as teachers as well as my own as investigator. What did I sacrifice? I had originally wanted to focus on the international students in the course: My concern lay with fostering much more individual accountability within the teams, and I thought that was an especially important issue for international students. Elizabeth Cohen influenced my thinking here. She writes that you have to make every member in the group perceive every other member as a resource; no one can succeed unless everyone succeeds. I had hoped, for example, that in every class period the professor would call randomly on a member of each team to report on the status of the team project, which meant that everybody on the team would have to be well informed enough to report to the class. But because the collaboration on project development had taken much of my colleagues' and my time to develop, too much of the quarter had passed to implement this idea effectively. The collaborative approach held this disadvantage.

Another downside was that I missed out on the richness that I heard from my fellow Carnegie Scholars when they presented their findings. So much of what was exciting in their work came from getting closer to the experience of their students, doing interviews with them, focus groups, and so forth. I didn't have that opportunity. The impersonality I had pursued in order to gain more scientific rigor had a cost, namely that I was not immersed in the community of the course. As one solution to this dilemma, one might look at Donna Duffy's approach. Donna's scholarship of teaching project (described elsewhere in this volume) entails a careful examination of her own practice and her own students' learning, but in order to get some of the data she needed, she partnered with a colleague—an anthropologist—who came in and observed the class. This brings a neutral third party perspective to bear, while at the same time enriching Donna's work by adding another discipline's perspective on the course.

Adapting Donna Duffy's idea of involving an outside observer, I find myself imagining that in my program, for instance, where we have something like twelve sections of this course offered every year, we might assign one person the job of paying attention to it, gathering information, reflecting on it, thinking about how it might be improved. And we might build that role and process right into the course design. But for now the investigation is in my hands.

Gathering the Evidence

Originally I had hoped to gather data midway through the quarter, at the point when the teams typically give each other feedback about their projects in progress. But because the project design was new, the schedule of activities varied from previous quarters, and I missed out on that first opportunity to collect data. This happens, I suppose, when you're trying to do something new and also study that new thing simultaneously—which is often what we're doing in the scholarship of teaching and learning. In any event, I did my data collection at the end of the quarter, after the team projects had been turned in.

In addition, I enlisted the cooperation not only of the two faculty who were trying the new project but also the other team teaching that quarter as well, whose students were assigned the original team project. I needed to gather data in both settings in order to have a comparison. Actually, there were four settings, since both versions of the course were taught in two sections, a day and an evening. At the end of the quarter I went into all four of the sections and asked the students to fill out two paper-and-pencil scales. I've done this kind of survey research since my graduate education, so I'm pretty comfortable with it. It's a typical way for somebody in the field of management or organizational behavior in particular to collect data.

> "At the end of the quarter I went into all four of the sections and asked the students to fill out two paper-and-pencil scales. I've done this kind of survey research since my graduate education. ... It's a typical way for somebody in the field of management or organizational behavior in particular to collect data."

The first scale was a measure of the student's perception of the effectiveness of his or her team. I went about gathering ideas for that survey by posting an inquiry on the Organizational Behavior Teaching Society electronic bulletin board, asking if anyone had scales that would serve this purpose. I got a number of responses, including one from Carnegie Scholar Larry Michaelsen's teaching assistant, who said she would send me the instruments that Larry has used in his research on this topic. Oddly, none of the things I received was quite what I wanted; they focused more on how students grade one another than on my question about overall team effectiveness.

Ironically, it turned out that one of my colleagues down the hall in the Marketing Department had just what I was looking for. He and two other colleagues published a paper in the *Journal of Management Education* wherein they evaluated how students in our MBA program felt about the team projects used in that program. And they had developed a scale for that purpose. So I borrowed that scale and added several items to more fully reflect the conceptual framework I was using. This scale worked beautifully. It has a very high reliability. It factored nicely. It's a scale worth sharing with people (Bacon, Stewart, and Silver).

I also developed a second scale, from scratch, to measure student perception of the roles they played in their team—task, maintenance, and self-centered roles, which is a fairly common framework in the team and group literature. In fact, the students had written a paper in the course wherein they reflected on the roles they played, so they were already familiar with these terms and distinctions. The purpose of the second scale was to find out whether students played different roles in the redesigned project than were prevalent previously. It ended up including a few bizarre items, such as "I delayed the group process by taking care of my own needs." I can't imagine anyone would answer yes to that. That scale didn't work particularly well. The reliabilities were marginal, so I didn't give much credence to the results.

Next I coded and analyzed the data from these two scales, which included the name of the team to which the student belongs (each team was required to name itself). This allowed me to analyze data by teams. I had the Statistical Package for the Social Sciences (SPSS) on my computer and I coded the data myself and entered it on an Excel spread sheet.

And then I used the SPSS program to analyze the data, starting with a one-way analysis of variance, a fairly robust statistical analysis for something like this. Using this method, I tested to see whether team effectiveness differed between the treatment section, where I had changed the group process, and the control group, where it stayed the same. I also looked for the mean of those four groups because analysis of variance doesn't tell you anything about mean differences, which interested me because I thought there might be a confound with time of day. The means in the treatment group were higher for both the day and evening sections but the mean in the day section control group wasn't much lower than for the day section of the treatment section, so I wanted to make sure that the effect wasn't caused by the dissatisfaction of the evening control section. To examine this possibility I did a two-way analysis of variance, which allowed me to enter the time of the class as an independent variable. I found no interaction, meaning that a main effect really did result from the changed project on team effectiveness.

I also did the same analyses on student perception of the roles played within teams, which revealed nothing significant at an acceptable level. The one thing that *did* turn up in these analyses was that members of a number of teams in the treatment section reported a slightly greater tendency to play maintenance roles in their groups. But since this was at the .07 level of significance, which is marginal, and since the scale's reliability was marginal in the first place, I didn't really focus very much on that. It's something I might look at if I could do more work on the scale in the future.

In addition to these statistical analyses of student data, I wanted to find out more about my colleagues' experience as teachers. Shortly after the end of the quarter I sat down with each of the two professors separately. (There was no method to this arrangement; I would have been happy to talk to them together but it just wasn't meant to be.) I asked each to talk about the new project—how it felt, what it was like…. This kind of qualitative approach is not such comfortable ground for me. I have collected data by interview in the past, but usually in quite structured ways— more or less "talking scales." These interviews, in contrast, were much more open ended. I had a set of questions but I pretty much let the conversation go where it went.

I followed this same procedure with both of my colleagues and found that they were extremely pleased with the new project. One cost was that they spent more time with the students, but they felt that it was productive time rather than the wheel-spinning of previous semesters.

I also interviewed the two professors who had used the original project design. Interestingly, they told me they hoped they could use the new project design next time. They knew about it and saw it as a positive change. But that leads to another unexpected lesson from my project—an ethical issue.

Ethical Issues

People like Thomas D. Cook and Donald T. Campbell write about the ethics of quasi-experiments in the field in which a favorable good is given to treatment sections but withheld from the control section. That's really an interesting ethical dilemma, one that I danced around in this project without much thought until it was over. The two professors in the control section could have benefited from the redesigned project, and in the end they felt their class evaluations had suffered because they hadn't used it.

So, apparently, did their students, who asked why they couldn't have used the new project. In fact, during the continuation of the course in the summer, many students from the control section jumped ship and changed to the treatment section, which, ironically, only punished the treatment professors for their success by giving them large sections. And of course the faculty left with the small sections also felt punished, as they were embarrassed by the mutiny.

These kinds of ethical issues are much on my mind these days. Because I'm director of scholarship in my college and we give out small grants for faculty to do scholarly projects, including the scholarship of teaching, I'm now looking more and more at the issue of students as subjects and the kind of permission needed to do this work. Faculty studies of their own classes make up the majority of the projects we've funded, which potentially puts things on uneasy ground. Say, for example, I create a new project for my course—such as this new team project—and then I have my students evaluate it. If they say they don't like it, there's at least the perception that this might count against them when I give grades. Students in these situations are by definition subjects at risk.

So where does informed consent come in when you're studying your own students? It makes me very nervous that we may not think of our students as subjects at risk when we collect data from them. This is an issue I've kept on my back burner, but that's not where it should be. It deserves discussion and thought by those of us doing the scholarship of teaching and learning.

Conditions for Doing the Scholarship of Teaching and Learning

One of the things that makes this work possible is that that my college has adopted a version of the Boyer model—which means that the notion of the scholarship of teaching is very much part of the fabric of not only my life but my colleagues' lives.

Secondly, my field—organizational behavior—makes it easy to focus on the class-room. The scholars in the discipline tend to hold a practice-what-you-preach ethos. When I talk to my students about motivation or performance appraisal or leader-ship, they look at what I model about those concepts in the way I manage the course. That is, the classroom is the most visible organization that the students and I share. Looking at the classroom analytically is completely in keeping with what I do as a scholar. There's a literature to draw on, a theoretical base. That helps a lot.

Financial support is, I know, an issue for some faculty doing the scholarship of teaching and learning. For me, such support is primarily symbolic. The amount of money we receive as Carnegie Scholars is about what I would have received by applying for an internal research grant. Did I need that money? In one sense I did, because it's a way of saying this work is just as important as work being done in more tradi-tional research contexts. But I have often found ways to do tra-ditional research without much funding. In fact, I've done presentations at my professional association meetings about how to do "cheap research." I've done my scholarship of teaching in the same way. I copied the questionnaires on our departmental copier. I already owned the software I needed to do the statisti-cal analyses. I could have hired a graduate student to enter the data but it would have taken longer to train the person than to do it myself, which I did. The only money I spent was for a few books and resources.

> "For me, it's simply feeding two birds with the same bread: You're trying to make your courses as effective as they can be. Why not collect data and write up what you're doing so that others can benefit as well?"

What obstacles did I have to deal with? I can't really think of any. For me, it's simply feeding two birds with the same bread: You're trying to make your courses as effective as they can be. Why not collect data and write up what you're doing so that others can benefit as well?

Benefits of the Work

On a practical level, my teaching team and the students we teach got a better project. And that means that every quarter this project is used our lives are easier than they were. The previous version of the project was like having a corn on your little toe; it wasn't something that required major surgery. But it was certainly an irritant. So on a practical level it was absolutely worth doing.

There are benefits to my scholarship, too. The study of teams is central to my field. My scholarship of teaching contributes to what is known about how teams can be used in MBA courses and other higher education settings. It's also possible, I think, to extrapolate from what I learned about teams in the classroom to teams in other kinds of organizations.

Finally, there are benefits to my professional field. I'm speaking here as associate editor of the *Journal of Management Education*. The scholarship of teaching and learn-ing in my field has progressed beyond the reflective essay. We wouldn't accept an article that came in simply with the teacher's reflections about what worked, about why she found it useful to try some new thing. Those kinds of essays are now being returned with requests for other voices, and for data from students. What did they learn from this? How do you know they learned better than before? We're moving beyond the purely journalistic to the scholarly. What makes a contribution to our field has gone up a level, and I see my work as a step in this direction, a reinforcement of a direction we've been trying to take.

Lessons Learned

It's hard to give advice in the abstract, but I would urge people to find out early on in their career how this work is valued in their settings, and what its impact might be on performance appraisal. My current setting is very supportive, for instance, but my first job out of school was at a place with a very traditional research orientation. I remember my department chair calling me in after I presented my first paper at the Organizational Behavior Teaching Conference. "What is this, Cindi?" he said. "Is it research or is it teaching?" And I said, "Well, it's teaching." And what I did with that answer was shoot myself in the foot because teaching was never going to count there. The department thought it was nice that I cared about my teaching, and they were proud of me, but that's as far as it went. So my first piece of advice to faculty thinking about the scholarship of teaching and learning is to take an honest look at this issue. I don't mean that you wouldn't want to do it if it didn't count at tenure time, but if you knew that, you might figure out how to make a different kind of case for it. Or you might frame your questions in a way that link them more directly with other research interests.

I would also urge people to become familiar with the literature on teaching and learning—and not only in your own field. When I discovered the literature on cooperative learning at the K–12 level, I felt sort of foolish; I should have known that literature before. Similarly, there are faculty exploring problem-based learning, which is a close cousin of case-method teaching, about which there's a huge literature in my field. My point is that it's useful to search across disciplines and contexts for relevant literature and practice. It's useful and it's right. Many people get excited about the scholarship of teaching and learning and think they are the first ones to have pursued these ideas. It's important to pay homage, as we do in research, to what's come before.

Finally, I'd say start with your real questions about your own setting, and with what you're already doing.

REFERENCES AND RESOURCES

Bacon, Donald R., Kim A. Stewart, and William S. Silver. "Lessons from the Best and Worst Student Team Experiences: How a Teacher Can Make the Difference." *Journal of Management Education* 23 (1999): 467–488.

Cohen, Elizabeth. *Designing Groupwork*, 2nd ed. New York: Teachers College Press, 1994.

Cook, Thomas D., and Donald T. Campbell. "The Design and Conduct of Quasi-Experiments and True Experiments in Field Settings," *The Handbook of Industrial and Organizational Psychology*. Ed. Marvin D. Dunnette. Chicago: Rand McNally College Publishing, 1976. 223–326.

Johnson, David W., Roger T. Johnson, and Karl A. Smith. *Active Learning: Cooperation in the College Classroom*. Edina, MN: Interaction Book Company, 1991.

Katzenbach, Jon R., and Douglas K. Smith. "The Discipline of Teams." *Harvard Business Review* March-April (1993): 111–120.

Organizational Behavior Teaching Society. <obts-l@bucknell.edu> "Organizational Behavior Teaching Society electronic bulletin board." (April 1999).

A Chemical Mixture of Methods

Dennis Jacobs
Chemistry, University of Notre Dame

Dennis Jacobs

D ennis Jacobs is professor of chemistry at the University of Notre Dame, a Catholic teaching and research university with an enrollment of 8000 undergraduate and 2500 graduate students. Born in Los Angeles, California, Dennis did his undergraduate studies at the University of California at Irvine and earned a PhD in chemistry from Stanford University in 1988. He joined the faculty at Notre Dame in 1988 and has developed a research program to explore chemical reactions that are used in fabricating microelectronic chips. Dennis' passion for teaching has led him beyond the traditional lecture hall and laboratory to work with faculty in developing service-learning opportunities for students in science. The interview for this case study took place in March 2000.

I am engaged in a project to understand how "at-risk" college students learn general chemistry in an alternative design to the large lecture environment. To assess the impact of the revised pedagogical approach, I have analyzed test performance data, administered attitudinal surveys, run focus groups, videotaped students engaged in small-group problem-solving exercises, and analyzed how students fare in subsequent science courses. This mixture of research methods has provided a comprehensive, multidimensional view of student learning within the context of my course.

Framing the Question

Three or four years ago I began teaching a large general chemistry course with nearly 1000 students divided in four lecture sections. It was a traditional introductory science course, but for me it became a concern when my office hours for the course were dominated by students who were struggling. I found their stories very similar. Many of them had never seen material covered at this level; they had never learned the problem-solving process. They were caught off guard by exams that require not only knowledge but understanding. And after one or two of these exams, their fate was sealed. Facing the prospect of a D or F, and watching the drop date approach, they saw no alternative but to withdraw from the course.

And the problem was that they were not just dropping four credit hours. Because the course is a gateway to a number of majors, dropping it often meant a complete shift in the dream of a future they may have had for themselves for many years. Their career ambition was out the window because of a bad experience in the first six weeks of General Chemistry—a course that offered very little opportunity to grow and develop. My empathy went to these students, and I felt a responsibility to address what I saw as an injustice. We need to recognize that students come from very diverse backgrounds in high school and that some of them need help with the transition to deeper modes of thinking and understanding required at the college level. Our course was not meeting that responsibility.

It was out of this experience that I created an alternative version of the course. Targeting 250 students (one section) identified as at risk, I set about to see if I could create a more active learning environment where more students could succeed. As I began teaching the new version of the course, I found myself asking a lot of questions about what kind of learning was taking place, and whether it was effective or not. In the midst of this work, the Carnegie program became available, which helped me formulate the questions I'm now trying to pursue about the impact of cooperative learning and related strategies on the conceptual understanding, problem-solving ability, and self-confidence that students develop in the first year.

Finally, I should mention that an initial circumstance shaping my questions was a mandate from the College Council. When I proposed the course there was some resistance from people both inside and outside of my department who didn't think it was a good idea. In their view, one purpose of first-year courses was to retain only students with the highest probability of success, and so this group had reservations about helping the weaker students along, the view being that if resources are limited, our responsibility is to help the best students. With this in mind, one of the stipulations that the council put on me was that the course was on probation for two years, after which I was to report back with evidence to show that the methods employed were actually having a positive impact. So I had to design my work to provide to that council and to the administration in general evidence of a positive impact. Moreover, I needed to track the at-risk students after they left my course to see what path they took and whether they succeeded in science and engineering.

The Context: A Course in General Chemistry

First I need to explain the student population on which my scholarship of teaching focuses: I identified at-risk students on the basis of Math SAT scores, which I have found to be one of the predictors that correlates most closely with performance in the course. Where most students stumble is on the ability to analyze a problem and map out a solution, and that skill is tested to some extent through the math portion of the SAT. Chemistry course grades from high school are less predictive because there's so much variation in the quality of instruction. What we did, therefore, was to identify a cut-off point, below which one quarter of the student population scored—the equivalent of one lecture section. Although this wouldn't constitute an at-risk group on many campuses, here at Notre Dame students with Math SAT scores at or below 630 had only about a 40 percent chance of completing an entire year of the course with a grade of C or better. This contrasts with a 75 percent success rate for students scoring above 630 on the Math SAT.

The dean of First-Year Studies and I discussed how to communicate the target audience to students, and we decided the best strategy was to be up front. We let students know that the two versions of the course are equivalent in almost every way: The semester hours are the same, the same texts are used, and the tests are largely identical (so the level of rigor is maintained). But we also tell students that the alternative section includes a number of supplemental experiences. We describe the course in a way that highlights the positive nature of these experiences, and we indicate that it's designed for students with a Math SAT of 630 or below. Beyond that, it's up to students and their advisors to make a choice. Some students will be below 630 but feel they don't really need additional help; some are above the cut-off but believe they could benefit. So there's some blurring of the line, as advisors use their discretion in placing students.

My attempt to foster more effective learning entails a number of new dynamics in the course. Because it's large, most faculty teach it exclusively through traditional lecture. But in the new section, each lecture includes segments wherein I post conceptually based questions, which students discuss in pairs. Students also come together on a weekly basis to work in four-person teams to solve particularly challenging problems—problems no single student could complete in the requisite time, but on which the team can make major headway in about an hour.

We also increase the degree of accountability: Students have to come prepared and participate on a weekly basis. This is in contrast to the dynamic we're finding in the traditional course, where students have spotty attendance and tend to do very little until just prior to the midterm, at which point they cram for two nights in a row.

So we're trying to change out-of-class study habits and also add meaningful activities to the time we do spend together. It's pretty sobering to realize that a student in the traditional section could go through the entire fifteen-week semester and never have to speak a single sentence that involves chemical concepts. In the alternative section, we're trying to create multiple occasions each week during which students are asked to defend their ideas and articulate their understandings. Although it seems natural to transform the way we teach General Chemistry to all students, there were circumstances that made this problematic. First, we didn't know that the use of cooperative learning would bring positive effects, and we didn't want to take a risk with a thousand students. Second was an issue of resources. It takes more TA support to run the redesigned course because there are more breakouts and small groups to monitor. So we didn't want to commit these resources in all four sections until we had concrete evidence that this was the way to go.

Where did the ideas for pedagogical change come from? To tell the truth, I had no experience, either as a teacher or student, with the kind of active learning strategies I was exploring. But I'd heard about cooperative learning in various presentations, and had been reading some of the literature. I was inspired by the book *Peer Instruction* by Eric Mazur, a physicist at Harvard, who wrote on the use of concept questions. And Barbara Walvoord, who directs Notre Dame's Kanab Center for Teaching and Learning, moved me further in these directions.

Gathering the Evidence

My natural inclination as a scientist was to undertake this work with a control group design. However, that would have required two comparable sections, and the courses were intended to serve two different populations.

So we weren't in a position to create strict control groups, but at the same time I knew I had to demonstrate some kind of differential effects. The solution was to create what I call layered groups, with comparisons within the year and comparisons across years. Throughout a given year, I compared the test performance of at-risk students to non–at-risk students. As expected, the at-risk population had a lower test score average. I then tracked this test score differential over a four-year period. For the first two years of the study, all students learned in the traditional lecture environment. In the latter two years, at-risk students were enrolled in the alternative section while non–at-risk students were taught traditionally. This is not ideal—not the classic control group model I would like to have used—but it was the best we could do. I should also say that my fellow Carnegie Scholars encouraged me to think *beyond* a control group model, which I've done in a number of ways, focusing one area of my investigation on outcomes, and another on process.

In the outcomes category, we've relied a lot on test data. This meant that we needed common test questions—questions that appear on the test in both the alternative and traditional sections. We had maybe a hundred or more of these common questions over each of the past two years. In the first two years of the study, all students took identical exams because they were enrolled in the same course.

What this test-data archive looks like is scores for overlapping (common) questions for 4000 students over a four-year period, some of whom have taken the traditional course, and some of whom have been part of the alternative version. In addition to evaluating cumulative test score averages, I have been examining how students perform on individual test questions, classified according to various taxonomies. For example, one taxonomy would sort the test questions by the number of independent concepts a student must work with to successfully solve the problem. In general, students are less successful solving two- or three-concept questions than they are at single-concept questions. A different taxonomy classifies test questions as to whether they are purely conceptual, require mathematical manipulations, or ask students to predict qualitative trends. By comparing how at-risk and non–at-risk students perform in individual taxonomy categories, I am trying to identify relative strengths and weaknesses in their understanding. That's one line of inquiry.

Another thing I've done to get at outcomes is to look at retention statistics and patterns related to attrition. These are longitudinal data that track students through both semesters of this course and through various sophomore-level science courses. Do they stay in the same academic major? How do they perform in later courses— especially courses we've identified where a lot of students tend to congregate in their second year? And how do these patterns relate to the experience they had in General Chemistry? Do at-risk students show better retention rates in science and engineering if they have experienced cooperative learning approaches in their first year of college?

Our ability to raise these kinds of longitudinal questions results from a partnership with Notre Dame's Office of Institutional Research (IR), which has provided us with data for a population of about 4000 students over four years. There's a first-year student survey administered by IR with a few hundred questions, out of which we've identified about twenty-five that get at attitudes and perceptions that might be important to the chemistry course experience—things about parents' income levels, the advanced degrees their parents might or might not have had, gender, ethnicity, etc. Institutional research also provides data about later course taking, GPA for every semester, choice of major, and so forth. So we can correlate these things with performance on course exams, and on individual questions on those exams.

How this partnership with institutional research developed is an interesting story. Historically, the IR mission had been entirely focused on serving the administration. When I came along and I talked to the director about helping me with this quite different kind of work, she told me it might take a couple of months to get the data together; at that point I was only looking at 400–500 students. Two days later she called me back and she had completed the work because she got very interested in the topic. It turns out her daughter was taking the course. So that worked out nicely. But then, when I came back later wanting to extend the project to a much larger population, it took four to five months before anything happened. I finally brought this to the attention of the associate provost, who gave my project high priority—and then all the data came forward in a couple of weeks. What has happened since then is that the Notre Dame steering committee for the Carnegie Campus Program has made a strong case that one of the staff members in IR should dedicate about one quarter of his time to investigating problems or questions originating from faculty wanting to learn about what's happening in their courses. So it has created a great shift in available resources. We're still ironing out the details of how this will work, but it looks like it will be much easier for faculty to do these kinds of projects in the future.

> "Our ability to raise these kinds of longitudinal questions results from a partnership with Notre Dame's Office of Institutional Research (IR), which has provided us with data for a population of about 4000 students over four years."

The second component of my work focuses on process—that is, on what actually happens in class and how students experience the redesigned course. I'm doing this in three ways.

I ran four focus groups at the end of the fall 1999 semester. I'm not actually teaching the course this year, and that has been a plus and a minus. In fact, it's being taught this year by an instructor who is teaching one traditional section and one redesigned section, which means that although the course has a little different flavor this year (making comparisons with past years problematic), it also provides a nice basis for comparability between the two sections that might not otherwise be possible: same teacher, same text, same labs, same tests, but different methods for different populations. This, in turn, means we're focusing more on structure and design—on elements of the course that are robust, independent of the instructor. That's one plus to my not teaching it. The other advantage stems from the fact that I can look at the course from a more objective, third-party point of view. I can sit in on a lecture and no one knows who I am. Furthermore, I can look at the student experience in ways I couldn't if I were their teacher—for instance, with focus groups.

I'm doing a series of focus group sessions with a particular instructor's students from both sections. Two groups were composed of students from the traditional lecture course, and two groups contained students from the redesigned section. There were three to four students in each group, picked randomly from the much larger number who were invited to participate and willing to do so. Of course this resulted in some bias toward those who felt passionate enough about the course to commit the time.

Each focus group session lasted about an hour and a half. My questions addressed how they were learning, where they thought their learning took place, and why. I've tried to address the different learning environments that exist in the courses. That is, I asked specific questions about how students felt solving problems in groups or pairing off to discuss concept-based questions in lecture. I tried to explore differences in the way homework is dealt with: In the redesigned course they have homework that is collected and graded; the traditional course has homework problems that are simply recommended but not graded or collected. I was looking at these kinds of dynamics, trying to analyze the different elements in these two courses and how students thought their learning was enhanced or not by these various elements.

I chose to use focus groups to explore these questions because I thought it would give me access to the student experience in a way that would otherwise prove difficult. But I had no experience with this method. In advance, therefore, I did some reading about how to run a focus group—and what I read made me pretty apprehensive. Much of the literature is full of cautions about what not to do, and I was nervous that I was going to blow it, that somehow I was going to bias the group in the way I phrased my questions or by my body language.

But, in fact, I found the experience to be a very natural conversation, and I learned a tremendous amount. One of the things that may have made it successful was that the students didn't know me. I set it up so that students were initially contacted by a staff person in the department; they RSVP'ed to her, and contacted her to set a time. Then, at the time of the focus group, I showed up and introduced myself—without the title of professor, so they didn't know my role. If they asked I would tell them, but mainly they saw me as someone trying to help the department figure out how our courses were serving our students and how we could improve them.

Students were very frank with me. Some, for instance, confessed to "never opening the book" all semester. If I were their instructor, they would not have said that. My study benefited from being one step removed from the course. I heard some things I wasn't at all aware of, and I heard others that confirmed things I had long suspected.

The focus group experience also seemed satisfying for the students. In the areas where they had a particular gripe, they especially appreciated having someone listen. All I could do was nod my head and paraphrase to convey a sense of understanding; I obviously didn't take the role of respondent to their problems. But I think they appreciated the fact that somebody was interested in hearing their story.

The focus groups were audiotaped, and then I did "loose" transcripts, paraphrasing student comments. Based on the transcripts, I identified a number of issues I wanted to test on a larger population of students; I wanted to find out how widespread some of their perceptions and attitudes were. For this, I created pre- and post-semester survey instruments by adapting one I got from the Field-Tested Learning Assessment Guide (National Institute for Science Education, n.d.) and adding to it questions specific to our environment here.

I had done some surveying in past years, but in this particular fall semester we administered one survey at the very beginning of the semester and a related survey at the end. Each student had an identifying record number so we could correlate their responses at the beginning and end, and also with their performance throughout the semester—how they did on exams and on individual questions. As a result this survey has provided another data base. I haven't yet fully explored it, except to look at the distribution of answers on the survey. So far, these data tend to affirm many of things I heard in the focus groups, but they put a more quantitative spin on the picture. I can say, for example, that attitude x is shared by 80 percent of the class. So the survey has amplified many of the ideas that came out of the focus groups.

What I want to do and haven't yet done is to look at paired questions—pre and post—to see if there are shifts in attitude. For instance, some questions ask about the students' perception of science: Do they have a fairly naïve view that science is strictly a collection of facts about nature? Or do they see science as a process of asking questions and collecting data and drawing conclusions? I'll have the opportunity to look at shifts in perception about this. I'm also looking at shifts in their perception of workload—what, at the beginning of the semester, they thought they would have to do to get through the course with a particular grade, and what they report as their actual workload thirteen weeks later. Already I'm seeing dramatic shifts on this issue, which I'm now trying to reduce and capture in a succinct way.

Finally, I am analyzing survey responses to a series of questions that ask students where they think their best learning takes place (for example, in lecture, lab, small-group problem-solving sessions, etc.). I will look for a correlation between a student's survey responses and his/her test average or test improvement. A positive correlation would suggest that students are cognizant of the learning experiences that are most effective for them individually. I hope to learn from this analysis the degree to which students benefit from different components of the course.

The third element in my investigation of the learning process is videotape. We had a professional videographer come in and record student groups engaged in a number of cooperative learning activities. He might stay with each group for five or six minutes so we can see some of its dynamics: Does the group work pretty independently? What happens when the TA stops by? What happens when the TA leaves? We have video of many groups working on the same problem, and we have videos of

> "Do they have a fairly naïve view that science is strictly a collection of facts about nature? Or do they see science as a process of asking questions and collecting data and drawing conclusions? I'll have the opportunity to look at shifts in perception about this."

the same group working on different problems. We can use these tapes to examine how various elements of problem design affect the richness and focus of discussion, asking which kinds of problems lead to rich discussion and which to a more perfunctory division of labor to get the job done. So our inquiry here is quite separate from the characteristics of the particular teacher and focused more on design features that any teacher might use.

A second purpose of the videotapes is to help us figure out what characteristics of groups make some groups work really well together and others not work so well. A third involves the role of TAs. What kinds and degrees of intervention by the TAs are most conducive to group learning (for example, passive listening, Socratic questioning, identifying student errors, providing ideas for alternative approaches)?

Emergent Findings and Broader Significance

What's probably obvious is that we have an incredibly comprehensive set of data. One of the challenges of this project is how to reduce it effectively to some meaningful conclusions and results. It seems like every time I start to draw a conclusion I come up with another question that I'd like to answer first. I want to go back and sort through existing data in a new way, or gather new data. I have this inclination in my own traditional research as well: I'm constantly struggling to decide when I have learned enough so that I can draw robust conclusions and move to publishing the results.

My strategy for dealing with this challenge is to begin by creating mini reports on each of the areas of evidence. For instance, in the longitudinal study I will work for a while on analyzing the data about student performance in later courses; I'll work up a couple of graphs, and then write a few paragraphs summarizing what the data tell us. The result will be a three- to four-page mini report on what I learned about how students do in, say, biology after taking General Chemistry.

I'll then set that aside and create another mini report on what I learned from the surveys. And another on the focus groups, and so on. I now have folders of these mini reports, each of which addresses only one area or type of evidence. The next step is to integrate these reports and pull together what I've learned about some of the key underlying questions that I started out with.

Meanwhile, I'm aware that I need to do more reading before I can pull everything together and go fully public. I have examined the literature in a preliminary way. My sense so far, from the dozen or so articles I've found on cooperative learning applied to general chemistry, is that most studies don't really include much concrete evidence about impact on students. There are published data on the rise in student self-confidence, for instance, and our surveys support that finding. But I can't point to articles that have brought to the discussion the type of evidence that I think would convince peer scientists. That's the contribution I believe our study can make—with longitudinal data that show that down the road a year or two later we're finding maybe 40 percent more students are making it through later courses than would have made it through or did make it through in prior years.

Conditions for Doing the Scholarship of Teaching and Learning

Working with the Carnegie Academy staff and the other Carnegie Scholars has made an enormous difference, allowing me to see what is possible and not possible and to reframe my questions in a different way—to think much bigger than I had thought before and to broaden my perspective about the potential audience for this work. Initially I was thinking of local groups—a handful of people at Notre Dame, mostly administrators, who would look at this evidence as a way of deciding how to allocate resources. Now I'm thinking about a much wider audience that expands beyond this campus and beyond chemistry.

The recognition that comes with being part of a prestigious national program has also helped. That has opened doors on this campus. For instance, I was able to call on the Office of Institutional Research because the provost's office saw that this work was backed by the Carnegie Foundation and felt that we needed to respond accordingly by putting our best resources toward the effort.

My chair was very responsive in this way as well. When I applied to the Carnegie program, I had to answer a question on the application that asked about how the institution would support my work and help me find the time and opportunity to carry it out. When I brought that question to my department chair, he asked me what I had in mind. I wasn't sure, actually, but I was hoping for some kind of reduction in my usual responsibilities. And he suggested a one-semester release from teaching—which he didn't have to do; it was very generous. The tradition here in my discipline is that in addition to directing graduate research we teach one major course, often a large lecture course, and then usually some labs or seminars. But I have one semester off from teaching, and in the other I have only a graduate course, which entails a small enrollment. Some colleagues find it ironic that as I move deeper into the scholarship of teaching I'm actually doing less teaching, but I would claim it's important to have this time for analysis and reflection.

In terms of obstacles and challenges, one issue has been that much of my data (and this reflects my professional identity as a scientist) has been quantitative. That's where my comfort level has been, and it's also appropriate to my context in that I'm working with large numbers of students. But the challenge in this has been that I have no expertise in statistics. I've had to figure out how to make myself proficient. I read some books, and I'm still reading. And I found some useful software packages, including a traditional one in social sciences, SPSS. I'm still trying to sort out how to control for this and that, and to run correlations, but I've learned a lot. It would have been helpful to have colleagues whose expertise I could tap in this regard.

The good news is that I expect to have more colleagues to interact with over the next couple of years. The institution is creating a structure for work on the scholarship of teaching and learning, and we just funded six projects (with one to six investigators on each) for the next year or so. Part of the plan is that we will meet every month (and perhaps for a more sustained period at the initial stage of work), with different projects featured at each meeting. The team will present a progress report and receive feedback. So this will provide a local, parallel version of the Carnegie

Scholars Program. I'm very excited about the kind of community and collaboration that will develop in the years to come.

Benefits of the Work

I have been thinking about where this kind of work fits into my career, and whether it will have a continuing place. I find it very valuable. In the last six months, I've learned a lot more than in the previous twelve years about how my students learn and about how to create the kind of classroom climate it takes to facilitate that learning. My outlook has certainly changed, and so has my practice. I'm teaching a graduate course now, and I'm trying a pedagogical approach unlike any I've used before, inspired by what I have learned in working with a completely different population. I'm curious to see how various active learning strategies work with graduate students. As a result of my project, I have decided to give one-on-one oral exams rather than written exams, because I now believe there is no better way to assess student understanding in this graduate course.

> "In the last six months, I've learned a lot more than in the previous twelve years about how my students learn and about how to create the kind of classroom climate it takes to facilitate that learning. My outlook has certainly changed, and so has my practice."

If the question, then, is whether I will continue to examine and reflect on the learning taking place in the courses I'm teaching, the answer is definitely yes. But I know that the scholarship of teaching is more than that; it means making work public, seeking out review, and having others build on the work. And that has been a very time consuming and challenging task, to bring this work to a level consistent with the standards of peer review. Writing scholarly publications has required a lot more of my time than I would spend on personal reflection of student learning in my classes.

At one level I see that this activity enhances my teaching and correspondingly the degree of learning achieved by students in my classes. That is a good thing, and I will always do it. The more challenging question is whether I will continue with the intent of making this work public, aiming to enter into the larger discussion and peer review process. I see compelling reasons for doing it, but there are also competing demands for my time that I'm still sorting out.

At this point in my career, I feel pulled in a lot of different directions. I haven't yet prioritized them in terms of where I find the greatest degree of meaning and reward. In the microcosm here in my own department, traditional research is weighted very heavily, and we're struggling to allocate as much time as possible in that direction.

On the other hand I've really enjoyed my interactions over the last six or seven months with the Carnegie project, and I see a lot of value and reward in those activities. As I write this, I'm looking forward to presenting my findings at the national meeting of the American Chemical Society. This will be an opportunity to interact with other chemists and feel the waters: I want to see if that community values and appreciates this type of work—whether it is ripe for investment of larger amounts of time.

I imagine that my activity in the scholarship of teaching and learning will be cyclical. I'm investing a lot of time in this right now and I will continue until this particular project reaches some kind of closure. Then I may put my time and energy into something else, and come back to the scholarship of teaching at a later point. My own life pattern reveals cycles, where I focus primarily on one or two things rather than balancing three or four. The time I allocate to different projects varies from year to year.

Lessons Learned

One thing that was very helpful right at the beginning was to think in a much bigger framework than I was accustomed to. Interacting in an interdisciplinary spirit with many other scholars allowed me to see what was possible and to hear and learn about lines of questions that I had never thought about before.

Similarly, I wouldn't advise that one lock into a particular project design prematurely. In the spring before the first meeting with other Carnegie Scholars, I had my project focus and mission pretty clearly in mind. Then in June, when I started talking with others and seeing what they were doing, I rethought a lot of what I originally had in mind. I began to discover in more detail what the scholarship of teaching entailed, and I found myself asking, with others, What does it mean to gather evidence of deeper understanding? Assessment was something I had never dealt with prior to this project in any meaningful way. My point here is that it's good to stay open to new possibilities, to think about options and alternatives, and be willing to reframe the effort as your thinking evolves.

I would also say in hindsight that periodic conversations with others can be invaluable. Seize any chance to maximize those opportunities. One thing I haven't done much of—and I feel badly about it—is to carry on conversations with my fellow Carnegie Scholars between meetings, in part because I realize how busy everyone is. I don't want to burden them by asking them to spend time reading my work. On the other hand, I know they are generous people and interested in my project. So my advice is to set up those relationships early on and establish some shared understandings about the level of interaction sought by each.

Finally, a thought about audiences for the work. In framing questions and projects, it's important to begin with audience analysis, anticipating what questions will come to the readers' minds, what things they might be skeptical about. And this is complicated because there are several audiences one might try to reach. There's an audience of consumers of the scholarship of teaching and learning, who want to know what pedagogical methods work and how to make their own teaching more effective. We most often think of addressing faculty in our own discipline. But another audience consists of faculty already doing this kind of scholarship, who will look at a study not to learn innovative ways to teach general chemistry but for models of how to do this kind of scholarship. I think it's important to consider the ways we present our work in order to reach each of these different audiences. The scholarship of teaching and learning will emerge as a legitimate and valued academic activity only if we make the methods, results, and conclusions of our projects widely accessible and open to peer review.

REFERENCES AND RESOURCES

Mazur, Eric. *Peer Instruction*. Upper Saddle River, NJ: Prentice Hall, 1997.

National Institute for Science Education. (n.d.). "Field-Tested Learning Assessment Guide." <http://www.wcer.wisc.edu/cl1/flag/> (2000, August 3).

CASE STUDY 5

**For Better or Worse?
The Marriage of Web and Classroom**

T. Mills Kelly
History, Texas Tech University

Mills Kelly

Mills Kelly is assistant professor of history at Texas Tech University, where he teaches a variety of courses on modern European history, as well as courses on the intersection of history and new media. His research focuses on the rise of radical nationalism in Habsburg Central Europe and on how using hypermedia in history courses influences student learning. This research has been supported by grants from the Woodrow Wilson International Center for Scholars, The Carnegie Foundation for the Advancement of Teaching, the International Research and Exchange Board, among others. Mills is also chair of the board of directors of the Civic Education Project, an international organization promoting educational reform in Eastern Europe and the former Soviet Union. His PhD is from George Washington University. The interview for this case study took place in February 2000.

My project is an investigation of the impact of hypermedia on student learning in a history course. Using my Western Civilization course as my laboratory, I offered sections using hypermedia and sections using only print and compared student outcomes from each setting. My goal is to be able to answer my main question by analyzing whether and how students in the hypermedia sections acquired various skills and arrived at a deeper understanding of historical content, relative to their peers in the print-based section.

Framing the Question

Because I'm an historian, I have to start by telling a story. A number of years ago, I began using the Web in my teaching in a variety of small ways. Then, when I went to Grinnell College in 1997, I found the resources to do this more fully. For one thing, all my students had computers. I seized the opportunity to migrate all of my courses from a print format onto a Web site. I need to be very clear that I'm not referring to virtual courses, offered online only; my courses are hybrids in which many of the materials students work with are found online, but I also continue to have classroom contact with students. I use this hybrid format for a personal reason, which is that for me it's the interpersonal connection with students that is the fun part of my job. And I'm not seeking to prove that hybrid courses work better than entirely virtual courses; that's not an issue for me, and not the question I want to ask; I'm just not willing to leave the classroom entirely.

As I began teaching in this new hybrid way at Grinnell, my department chair, Dan Kaiser—who was supportive of using the Web in teaching and very interested in it—asked me a wonderful question over coffee one day: "You know," he said, "One question I wonder about is how you know that using the Web, as opposed to depending on paper (the way most of us have taught history), is transforming student learning—and, if so, whether for good or for ill?" And I said, "Well, I don't! I have no idea."

In fact, I had never asked that question before. I was teaching in new ways because I wanted to, because it was fun, and because the more I used the Web in my courses, the more my students seemed to respond positively. That is, I saw anecdotal evidence that they were becoming more engaged with the subject matter, and with me as an instructor. So I sensed a connection: The more I used the Web, the more they were engaged and therefore the more they were learning. Or at least they were learning differently in a way that seemed better.

But all of this said, I was stumped by my colleague's question. So that's how I got started—with a very pragmatic, instrumental question. If the answer to Dan's question over coffee was that my use of the Web caused students to learn worse, then I was wasting my time, which I couldn't afford to do.

The Context: An Historian's Perspective

When I began trying to answer Dan's question, I started by doing what historians do: I went to the library to look at the existing research. Given how much money we've spent wiring classrooms for the twenty-first century, I assumed that somebody had answered this question already. I found huge bibliographies on how teaching is changed, as well as a smaller listing of work on how the power relationship in the classroom is changed by the introduction of hypermedia. There's also a good deal of work in history focused on the debate over cultural literacy: What should students learn? Should they know that Thomas Jefferson was the third president of the United States? What facts should they know? Should they know something more than facts? This is a big debate but not, in my view, a productive one.

What I didn't find is much work on how students *learn* in any kind of history course, though Sam Wineburg's work is very good in this regard. And I found nothing, really, about the effect, positive or negative, of the use of hypermedia on students' learning of history. So this helped to sharpen my question.

It also made me realize that to figure out how my use of technology influenced students' learning, I first had to understand how their learning occurred at all—which has been a transformative experience for me. For the first time I began really thinking about how my students were learning—rather than worrying about the fact that I couldn't spend another hour talking about Napoleon. There never is enough time in a history course, no matter how precisely defined it is; you can spend an entire semester on the Battle of Waterloo and still feel like you've short changed students. So focusing more on how students learn, rather than on what does or doesn't get covered, has freed me from the tyranny of content.

At the same time, I began to realize that I didn't know much about how to formulate the question I wanted to explore. So when I moved to Texas Tech, I sat down with people in our Teaching, Learning, and Technology Center to ask for help and they told me that my investigation was an example of the scholarship of teaching. I'd never heard the phrase before. I'd have to say that at first the term intimidated me. I'm not an educational researcher by training. I'm an historian. And in the reading I had done to that point, I was running up against a methodology that I knew nothing about—a new language, a use of control groups, a scientific approach. And I realized that that tradition was just not something I was going to follow. I didn't have the training; it wasn't a good match for my background. So I told myself, OK, I'm not going to do something with a double blind and proper control groups—all the accoutrements of the scientific approach that an experimental psychologist would want to see. Historians don't do that. History is messy and uncontrollable, requiring that all historians, no matter how quantitative (and I do a lot of quantitative work), use qualitative approaches in their work. We're very comfortable with qualitative methods.

We're also very comfortable with qualifying our results. That is, I may work on a topic for ten years, and in the end I'll still use caution before I conclude anything with certainty. Historians are very good about revealing what they can't say as a result of their research. When you read the footnotes in academic monographs by good historians, often they will have reported on the problems with such and such a conclusion. We're good at this sort of work, and comfortable with it.

I can illustrate this point by talking about the idea of recursiveness. Recursiveness is important to historical understanding. Simply put, it's what historians do. When we're mucking around in this messy thing called the past we find something, some source, and often we have to read it and think about it dozens of times before we're willing to commit ourselves to one interpretation. We test that interpretation constantly against new information available to us when we get to the archive we haven't gotten to for years or when we have a revelatory moment and think about it in a different way. We go back to the same sources we've hashed over and over and over and over and finally produce something. That's one of the things that separates good historians from not very good historians: The good ones reflect on their research more carefully, and through multiple iterations. So I would posit that being recursive in the use of sources is essential to what good historians do and therefore a behavior we want to foster in students. And whether students engage in this behavior is something we can investigate, something we can learn more about.

> "So I would posit that being recursive in the use of sources is essential to what good historians do and therefore a behavior we want to foster in students. And whether students engage in this behavior is something we can investigate, something we can learn more about."

Gathering the Evidence

The main source of evidence for me was students, and I was very straightforward about this: I asked them a lot of questions. Students are remarkably honest if you establish a relationship of trust, I've found. Today for instance I asked how many had not done the reading for the day, and the ones who hadn't raised their hands. They may not be as embarrassed about it as they should be, but they're honest. Of course you can also design assignments that give students the opportunity to demonstrate that they've done the work (or haven't).

Additionally, at the end of the semester, I administered a survey, which included a question that asked, "Did you have occasion to go back to primary source documents assigned earlier in the semester, and if yes did you simply read them, or did you incorporate what you found into later assignments? How did doing this influence your thinking about material later in the semester?" The survey gave me general information about how the students used the various sources I provided to them, how they used the Web site, what role technology did or did not play in their learning process, and so on.

But I also wanted to get into more depth on some issues, and for this I decided to do in-depth interviews. I flagged five students, and this semester I'll interview five more, from each class, spread across the performance levels, that is a couple of A students, a couple C students. I chose students who had had different levels of success in the course because I wanted to see whether the technology had influenced their success in any way that I could determine in the interviews. My assumption is that students who earn lower grades are generally less satisfied with the course than students who earn an "A," so I was curious to know whether they were also dissatisfied with the use of technology (or lack thereof) in the course. Because I worry about research subjects anticipating some penalty or benefit from participating in something like this, all the interviews were conducted after my grades were turned in. I asked all five students the same basic set of questions, which revolved around my research question. My purpose is to explore what the survey alone could not tell me: not only how and whether students did assignment x but what they were thinking about when they did it.

So, for instance, when a student reported that she had in fact gone back to an earlier source when she was working on her final paper, I asked her why she did that, how she went about it, and whether she would have done the same thing if all the material had been in a course pack rather than on the Web. And, very interestingly, she said no to this last question. I was puzzled by this, and asked her to elaborate. She said, "Well, you know, all that paper is so cumbersome." This is a useful insight because this is a young woman who has used computers in the majority of her learning experiences over the past several years. For her, paper is now cumbersome, whereas if it's there on the Web, she finds it easier or more fun. That's not to be minimized. Furthermore, it's not something you can find out in a survey. What made the interviews especially helpful was that the students knew they were going to be interviewed. When they came in they knew I was going to ask questions about their experience over the course of the semester; they had really thought it through, and had thought about how they learned.

The interviews were a really wonderful experience. I hope to have the time to conduct them every semester for as long as I teach because I learned so much more about the course in the interviews than I did from teaching the course.

Emergent Findings and Broader Significance

I have begun to write about my emerging conclusions and presented a paper at the American Historical Association (AHA) meeting this past January, laying out some of what I think I'm finding. Two things are most notable, though still in the category of "tentative conclusions." First, my work seems to suggest that properly designed courses using hypermedia can in fact result in different learning by students than would be the case in a typical print-based course. Students in the hypermedia sections, as a group, produced essays that displayed a more sophisticated understanding of the historical evidence, and they spent more time researching their topics. But I'd add two qualifications right away. One is that the print course, if properly designed, might be able to accomplish the same things. I've never seen it done, but it's possible. David Pace (a fellow Carnegie Scholar in history) is doing research that may prove me wrong; he may find among the folks he's interviewing that there are faculty who can do this. But the issue is proper design—not technology; that's the qualification. A second qualification is that my students are from a particular setting and milieu: The majority come from rural West Texas and eastern New Mexico, typically from small and resource-poor high schools. Of course there is no such thing as a typical student. But it's possible that if I visited Brown University or Miami-Dade Community College or Alverno College, I might find different things. This is what I hope to do next, test my findings in other settings. That would give me greater confidence in my conclusions. To that end, I have applied to both the Spencer Foundation and the National Endowment for the Humanities for funding in order to expand my project beyond the confines of Texas Tech.

A second emerging conclusion is this notion of recursiveness. That is, my research demonstrates that students employing hypermedia are more likely to go back to earlier materials in the course; something about the online access to resources creates a disposition to engage in the recursive reading of sources. I've had to ask myself whether this is an important behavior, and how and why: What kinds of outcomes does greater recursiveness lead to? Meanwhile, my colleagues in this work are telling me that recursiveness is important (though in different ways) in fields other than history, as well, because it is related to the development of critical thinking.

I'm also discovering some things that are not really answers to my question as I originally formulated it—but that are very interesting. One of the questions at the end of my survey was, What was the most important thing you learned this semester? I got a response from close to 20 percent of the students that had not even occurred to me as a possible response (I thought I was asking a question about content): "I learned to take responsibility for my own learning." This was to me a real surprise. I thought they would say something about Marxism or the French Revolution.

This finding is not, I think, related to the use of the Web. It's more a function of pedagogy, of the way I taught the course, with writing assignments and collaborative endeavors, but no examinations. Today, for example, the students had to read one of several primary documents, and then I grouped them together and let them figure out what these documents meant and then report back to the group. The emphasis lay on student responsibility for making sense of complex material.

Finally, in thinking about the results of this work, I would also mention a sort of spin-off idea that I'm excited about. In my graduate readings course last semester, the students especially liked the fact that instead of coming into class and giving the typical report about the book they read for that week, they posted their one-page synopsis on line. At the end of the semester I made and gave to each student a CD-ROM of that discussion archive. When they get ready to take their comprehensive exams they can go back to that extensive bibliography and reacquaint themselves in fairly short order with all the books read and reported on during the semester rather than trying to resurrect from their notes what someone said about such and such a book.

Conditions for Doing the Scholarship of Teaching and Learning

In terms of published literature, Samuel S. Wineburg was probably my biggest help—and Howard Gardner. I see them as approaching the same question from slightly different vantage points; both talk about a mode of learning that is actually very unnatural. Wineburg has a wonderful article about historical thinking being an unnatural act, and Gardner says many of the same kinds of things, pointing to the fact that we have built into our minds by age five ways of thinking that run counter to our schooling. In other words when we encounter something new we revert to thinking like five-year-olds. Reading Wineburg and Gardner's work, I realized that students don't know much about how to learn about the past. History teachers in high school and in college haven't done much to help them. This is one of the reasons we don't know much about how students learn.

Wineburg's work was also helpful in its method. His study—the one reported on in the *Phi Delta Kappan* article—does not pretend to draw conclusions about the teaching of history in general. Instead, Wineburg focuses on what can be called "best practices." He begins by identifying teachers who seem to be getting it right; he starts there, with questions about what they're doing, and why it seems to be working so well. Thus, rather than examining all forms of history teaching, Wineburg focuses in on several "best" examples, and asks why students seem to "get it" so well in those courses, and why, even in exemplary classes, there are still gaps in their learning that are obvious to the critical observer. He also gave experienced historians the task of analyzing primary source documents, either things familiar to them or items related to their field of expertise. And he analyzed how they thought about the material and thought about how students thought about the material.

Wineburg's work became an important context for my own because it was clearly research, but it was very qualitative and didn't pretend to be a scientific sample. Yet he was able to draw some very powerful conclusions. This said to me that it would be possible to draw some similarly powerful conclusions, properly qualified, from my setting with a limited sample. He gave me permission to do this work as an historian.

Three of the Carnegie Scholars were also especially influential, though in very different ways. The first is Bill Cutler, a fellow historian who is, as I am, looking at questions related to technology and the use of primary sources in the teaching of history. Looking at Bill's work helped me to sharpen my own questions, realizing that mine were actually different from his.

A second very helpful influence has been Mariolina Salvatori, whose work focuses on students' "moments of difficulty." Her field is English but she has been asking some of us from other fields how we think about this topic. She got me thinking about how hard it is to create experiences for students that are just difficult enough to open a door that the student and the instructor can walk through together, as opposed to being just a brick wall. So her approach helped me think about course and assignment design and where technology fits in. One of my goals is to figure out how to create the circumstances whereby my students would ask the kinds of questions that would open up bigger questions. This is hard to do.

> "Wineburg's work became an important context for my own because it was clearly qualitative and didn't pretend to be a scientific sample.... He gave me permission to do this work as an historian."

The third person was Susan Nummedal, a psychologist, because it was she who finally gave me permission to let go of the scientific paradigm, to stop worrying about meeting the standards of a field that is not my own, and to do the work in a way that makes sense in my own scholarly community.

What conditions made my work more difficult? I think I made a mistake by not figuring out on the front end how to turn what I'm doing into something to be celebrated in my own department. I say this not because I want the personal gratification of receiving pats on the back by my colleagues but because I wish that my colleagues could actually engage with what I'm doing, and find it worth thinking about. For instance, the department is now struggling with the issue of assessment; I have an undergraduate studies committee meeting coming up, and I'm going to propose a method for assessing student performance in introductory history courses based on some of my research. I suspect some of my colleagues are going to be uneasy about this, and skeptical. Because my questions clearly involve assessment, I think the department could make more progress had I figured out on the front end how to engage others with the question of student learning. I didn't do this because I think I was consumed with trying to get my own project started. I was—I now realize in hindsight—operating pretty much behind a closed door. So that's one thing I'd do differently, because I think there's an audience for the work beyond the campus, but if my own department isn't affected, it would be a shame.

Benefits of the Work

The work reported here is tremendously enjoyable. I've been having a wonderful time doing this, and whether or not I turn out anything that others will find useful, the process of constantly thinking about how my course is designed and delivered—and what it leads to for students—has certainly made me a better teacher, and, I would say, a better scholar. But I would also point to the fact that this year my students have more to say in class, that they're more excited about the material. This morning for example: I teach two sections consecutively in the same classroom. Ten students arrived early for the second session. Outside the door they were talking about course materials so vigorously I had to step outside and ask them to keep their voices down. To me that's a sign that it's working.

But on the flip side, the scholarship of teaching presents a real danger for early-career academics. And that is that it's fun. It provides a lot of instant gratification in a profession where gratification is typically down the road. I work on this course, and I see my classes changing, my students getting more engaged. I've been invited to make presentations on the scholarship of teaching at two campus colloquia and I've been invited to visit other campuses, as well. But the scholarship of teaching can easily divert me from longer-term work on my book. So it's important to be very disciplined. On Tuesdays and Thursdays I'm not allowed to think about teaching; I have to work on the book that will get me promoted. If I were tenured none of this would be an issue.

Lessons Learned

I'd urge colleagues interested in the scholarship of teaching to begin by identifying where the resources are to help do the work. I sort of missed this step because, frankly, I didn't realize there were resources and a community I could tap into. Or rather, I turned to the research but I neglected to find the people. The best advice I have is that you don't need to invent this all by yourself. Find people doing similar work.

Some of those people—many of them—are not here on my campus, but even here it's getting easier. Texas Tech has a new Teaching Academy, which has a proposal in front of the provost to add to the existing distinguished professorship for research a parallel distinguished teaching professorship. This will get people's attention because it has the same large salary bump added to your base. That piques people's interest.

Second, I advise people to deal with the issue of time. Money is nice and monetary awards cause people to pay attention, but release time is even more important, in my experience. Unless you teach a reduced load (by Texas law I have to teach three organized courses a semester), the scholarship of teaching is an optional activity. To do it, and to do it well, requires time, and time is harder to come by than cash.

REFERENCES AND RESOURCES

Gardner, Howard. *The Disciplined Mind*. New York: Simon and Schuster, 1999.

Gardner, Howard. "Educating the Unschooled Mind." The Science and Public Policy Seminar Series, American Educational Research Association, Dirksen Building of the US Senate. Washington, DC, 14 May 1993.

Gardner, Howard. *The Unschooled Mind*. New York: Basic Books, 1991.

Wineburg, Samuel S. "Historical Thinking and Other Unnatural Acts." *Phi Delta Kappan* (March 1999): 491.

Wineburg, Samuel S. "Models of Wisdom in the Teaching of History." *Phi Delta Kappan* (September 1998): 50–58.

Wineburg, Samuel S. "Picturing the Past: Gender Differences in the Depiction of Historical Figures." *American Journal of Education* 105 (February 1997): 160–185.

Wineburg, Samuel S. "Probing the Depths of Students' Historical Knowledge." *Perspectives* 30, 3 (1992): 19–24.

Wineburg, Samuel S., and Janice E. Fournier. "Reading Abraham Lincoln: An Expert/Expert Study in the Interpretation of Historical Texts." *Cognitive Science* 22, 3 (1998): 319–346.

Students' Perspectives on Interdisciplinary Learning

Sherry Linkon
English and American Studies, Youngstown State University

Sherry Linkon

Youngstown State University is an open-enrollment, urban state university, serving a five-county area in northeastern Ohio and western Pennsylvania. Most of its 12,000 or so students come from this area, and many live at home, sometimes driving as much as an hour to get to class. Nearly all of them work at least one job, and a good number are over thirty and have families in addition to full-time jobs. Most YSU students come from working-class backgrounds and are the first generation of their family to go to college.

Sherry wears several hats at YSU. She's professor in the English Department, teaching composition, literature, and occasional courses in theory, as well as courses in the Departments of American Studies and Women's Studies. As coordinator of the American Studies program and co-director of the Center for Working-Class Studies, she works with students and colleagues across the boundaries among disciplines. Sherry's PhD in American Studies is from the University of Minnesota. The interview for this case study took place in February 2000.

This project explores students' experiences in interdisciplinary courses, especially their understanding of the concept of interdisciplinarity. Through surveys, focus group interviews, ethnographic interviews with several students, and examination of student work in three courses, I am gathering data on students' attitudes toward interdisciplinary courses, how they explain the course process, how they define interdisciplinarity, the difficulties they encounter, and their ability to integrate methods, materials, and ideas from several disciplines in their own projects.

The Context: Interdisciplinary Learning

What really launched my project was the Carnegie program on the scholarship of teaching. I had been teaching interdisciplinary courses for a long time. Then, a few years ago, I started working with some colleagues to design a new version of an interdisciplinary course that we would all teach, and I felt like I should be the "resident expert." But I certainly didn't always feel like I had good answers to the challenges posed by interdisciplinary teaching. The Carnegie program call for proposals made me stop and think about what questions I really needed to explore.

One influence on my thinking was that I had done a fair amount of work—I wouldn't quite call it research but a lot of interaction and mentoring—in composition. I had always been intrigued by the body of work in composition aimed at getting inside students' heads, trying to understand how people learn to write by closely observing the writing process. Scholars in composition studies have worked from the premise that we need to know much more about what students do when they write; they bring ethnographic approaches to bear on these questions. The idea is to move from a focus on the final products of writing to understanding more about how those products develop. A related shift meant focusing less on what teachers know and more on what students do. I had the sense that a similar shift would be powerful for interdisciplinary courses.

I asked myself why interdisciplinary studies hasn't already done the kind of work I'm imagining. Faculty have published a lot of teaching stories, wherein the teacher tells about what she taught, how she taught it, what happened, and how the students liked it. These are wonderful stories, but they don't necessarily get us to a deeper understanding of what's going on for students. So I started with that.

The next stage in my thinking—it felt like a real vision-changing experience—came through the assignment in the Carnegie application guidelines to select and write a commentary on a student work sample. I had written a few articles and edited a book on teaching, but amazingly I had never sat down and looked closely at a piece of student writing as a "window" on the learning process. So I pulled out a student's final essay from my fall quarter literature class, and I was surprised to realize how much she had struggled with the task of linking history and literature. We'd been working on it all quarter, but in her final paper, this student didn't seem to be able to make the connection. Instead, she did more "standard" literary things, like focusing on the text itself and suggesting that the author's individual experiences might account for her ideas. Interdisciplinary thinking seemed to be very hard for this student, and I didn't know if it was because she was an English major, and maybe she'd learned the practices of that discipline fairly well already, or if the task simply felt confusing or daunting.

When I tried to map out this dilemma in a reflective memo, it became very clear to me that I could only know so much of what was going on. I needed to sit down and talk to the student, to find out more about what she was thinking when she wrote the paper. And of course I didn't have her there to do that so I could only make guesses. As a result, I became convinced very quickly of the limitations of any effort to study how students were learning without talking to students.

So I came to the idea of adapting the ethnographic approach, coming from composition studies. I saw this as a chance not only to learn more about interdisciplinary studies but also to explore methods for understanding more about the student learning process. Part of my goal is to experiment with different approaches, to see whether I like them, to see what I get from them. I anticipate doing a lot of playing around this year.

Framing the Question

Many faculty are excited about teaching interdisciplinary courses. And students often report that they enjoy them. But I wasn't sure what students or faculty thought was really going on. Interdisciplinarity is something lots of people do, or purport to do, but we don't always think carefully about it. So that was part of it. Moreover, I had a sense, partly from talking to students, partly from looking at their work, and partly from talking to colleagues, that students were having a difficult time doing the things we asked them to do. Interdisciplinary work is *complicated*. We ask students to look at four or five different kinds of things and then somehow to synthesize those, which is a pretty high-level cognitive task. I was curious about how students do this and particularly about whether students need to be self-conscious about inter-disciplinarity in order to engage in it effectively. I've taught courses where I never breathed the word "interdisciplinary," but students did lots of interdisciplinary work, and I've also taught courses where I was very explicit about drawing from history and sociology and literature. So one of my questions is about the conse-quences of being explicit, or not.

This is an issue that spills over beyond interdisciplinary studies to all areas of study. How explicit do we need to be with students? Do students need to know what a theory is, what a model is? Do they need to understand the concept of paradigm in order to be able to work with one? Or can they make use of those ideas without necessarily having a clear concept for them?

I also wonder about how to stage the discussion about interdisciplinarity in the classroom. When is the right time? How should we do it? One of the arguments that people make about interdisciplinarity is that it's a more natural way of thinking about things; that nobody encounters the world in disciplinary boxes. On the one hand that suggests that interdisciplinary thinking ought to come easily, because it's natural, but I'm skeptical about the idea that anything is essentially natural—as if you had some innate interdisciplinary model of the world. It certainly is the way people experience their lives, but just because it's what we do all the time doesn't mean that we can articulate the experience. You ask someone to explain how to wash your face. Here's something we do without ever thinking about it, and stop-ping to explain it is hard. But if you're a biologist studying the spread of bacteria, you might really need to know the nitty-gritty of facial hygiene. At what point do people become conscious in this way? What happens or can happen to move things to a self-conscious level?

One thing I'm trying to find out is if students struggle to do interdisciplinary things because they've already learned disciplines or because they haven't. When I sat down to analyze that student sample I noticed that the student seemed to be falling back into habits that looked like those used in a standard literature paper. And I thought, well, maybe she's learning the English discipline so well—it's become so safe or habitual—that it's an obstacle. Part of what I'm trying to do is figure that out.

The first stage of my research involved doing some surveys and talking with faculty in some courses that use interdisciplinary approaches. In one of those courses, the faculty member was very overt about explaining interdisciplinary studies and how her interdisciplinary literature course was going to be different from other literature courses because the class would be doing things that come from other disciplines. But another colleague teaching a similar course never explained these distinctions at all. And I don't sense that students in those two classes had different levels of understanding at the end. So it may not matter. Maybe this is not even the right question. The better question may be about how to model interdisciplinary ways of thinking.

> "Looking at how students learn interdisciplinary ways of thinking can help us teach that mode of thinking more effectively. This isn't about the best methods but about understanding the complicated stuff that goes on in teaching and learning."

Finally, I should say something about what questions I'm *not* interested in exploring. There's a long-standing debate about whether students need to understand the disciplines in order to move to interdisciplinarity. But my sense is that it's an old discussion. It's not unrelated to my questions, but it's not the debate I want to get into. Nor am I interested in proving that interdisciplinarity is better in some way than learning within traditional disciplinary boundaries. Interdisciplinarity is all over the place—in general education, new programs, and even within the disciplines. So I don't know that the better-or-worse question gets anybody anywhere. Certainly I don't want to suggest that disciplinary courses don't have an important place.

I don't think scholarship of teaching should be about creating normative models, the one right or best way to teach. Rather, my goal is to explore something that I know a lot of people are doing and to try to identify some general things that can help us do that thing better. My focus isn't on how we should teach but on how students learn. Looking at how students learn interdisciplinary ways of thinking can help us teach that mode of thinking more effectively. This isn't about the best methods but about understanding the complicated stuff that goes on in teaching and learning.

Gathering the Evidence

The tradition of ethnography is that you study members of a cultural group in order to get a sense of their culture. People in composition have adapted the method, not with the idea that you're going to get a sense of students' culture, but in order to understand their experience *as students*. For my project, I decided to focus on the experiences of students in an upper-division American Studies course taught by one of my colleagues. I took some surveys and gathered samples of students' work, and I conducted a focus-group type interview with the whole class. But the most important data gathering took place during a series of interviews with three students in the class, over the course of the quarter. I asked the interviewees to try to tell me what was going on in that class and in their heads, how they wrote a particular paper, how they saw things. In keeping with the tradition of ethnography, I tried not to impose my model of how things work but, rather, to get the interviewee to reveal the way he or she sees the world. I think this is a right method for my interests because there's almost no way on a survey, on an analysis of a piece of student writing, or even simply while watching a class that I can put myself into students' consciousnesses. In any class students try to make sense of things—of what's going on and what's important. I hoped that these interviews would give students a chance to reveal that process.

I started by asking a very open-ended question: what is the course like? From there, I asked for more description and examples, and I asked how they felt about the experience. The student might say, "Well this is a course in ethnicity in America" (that's one I'm working on during the spring of 2000), and then I'd ask, "What do you mean by that, what *is* ethnicity in America? How are you studying it, what are you looking at?" So the first interview started out very open ended, very dialogic, with follow-up probes, requests to explain…. One of the things ethnographers do is to begin creating categories out of what they hear, and then using those categories to ask further questions. They also check to see if they are understanding what's said: *I think this is what you've told me but am I getting that right? What am I missing in understanding this?* The interviewer can prompt people to correct and fill in gaps. In the second and third interviews, then, I asked again about some of the things we discussed in the first round.

I never started the interviews by asking about interdisciplinarity. I asked about it, but not until the end. That helped me to get a sense of how students saw it. What was interesting is that all of the students I interviewed thought that the course was very different from others they had taken, and they even talked about how this course was different from other courses in history or literature. They described pretty well how interdisciplinarity works, but they didn't use that term. One of my goals was to find out if interdisciplinarity would come up without my prompting. When I finally asked them to define "interdisciplinary," their responses varied pretty widely.

I did three sets of interviews: one during the first half of the quarter, one while the students were working on a paper, and one during finals week, when the course was finished. In later interviews, I asked the kinds of open-ended "tell me about the course" questions I've already mentioned and also questions about what students were doing, the assignments, the papers, the reading…. What do you do with a reading, why do you think you're reading that, what is the point? How do you relate it to this other thing? I wanted to keep my questions as open as possible. Importantly— and probably reflecting my literature background—I wanted students' own words. I was especially interested in seeing how their explanations of the course changed from week two or three to the end.

I interviewed all of the students who volunteered—only three out of eleven students in the class. Some fields would see a problem here with representativeness. But I'm much more interested in getting a good body of qualitative information than with proving that it applies to everyone. I got lucky, because I had the chance to interview students from three different fields—an American Studies major, an English major, and a political science and philosophy double-major. This gave me some interesting insights, but all three of the volunteers were students who defined themselves as "unusual" thinkers. That is, all three of them said that they tend to be more curious and questioning than other students. I wish I'd also been able to interview at least one student who found the course less comfortable, just to see if a clear difference would surface.

One thing that really helped with this project was working with two colleagues—the woman who was teaching the American Studies course and one of the people whose class I surveyed in the fall. All three of us were teaching interdisciplinary courses during the spring of 2000, and they were interested in learning more about how to do research on students' learning. So we ran some surveys in all three courses, we all kept copies of our students' papers to review later, and we went into each other's classes to conduct focus group interviews. This way, we could compare our experiences and perceptions and get information from more students.

We did a survey around mid-term time, asking students how they would describe the course and how they were working with the course materials. We used these as an entry-point for the focus group interviews. For the focus groups, each of us went into one of the other classes and interviewed the whole class. We asked students to describe the course (as in the individual interviews, we wanted to get students' words, to find out how students would explain the course focus and approach), to talk about how the course is similar to or different from other classes, how easy or difficult the course was, and how the ideas in the course related to other classes. All of these interviews were taped, so we can review the responses carefully as we move toward analyzing our classes. We did another survey at the end of the course, asking for an overall evaluation and focusing on what made the course challenging.

In addition to the strategies already mentioned, I did several things to fill in the picture. First, I developed a preliminary baseline questionnaire for my own class—a cousin to the instruments developed by two of my fellow Carnegie Scholars working on questions about interdisciplinarity. The questionnaire is a first stab at learning how students think about and understand interdisciplinarity. One question asks them to tell me what a discipline is; another asks what they think it means that a course is categorized as interdisciplinary. Their responses were mixed, about half and half, between students who had a pretty clear idea of what these terms meant and students who had no idea or a completely wrong idea.

Additionally, the campus is doing a much larger survey of about 2000 students—about 10 percent of YSU's undergraduate population—asking them about their experiences in several kinds of courses, including interdisciplinary courses. There are questions about how many courses they've taken, which ones, what they found helpful. … Interestingly, students developed and are administering this survey. The first round of this survey has already been completed, and we found that only about 200 out of 900 students said that they had taken an interdisciplinary course. We'll be getting the rest of the data soon, which will give us an even larger population for testing our findings.

At the end of this process we will have one pool of data that will cover sixty students in three different interdisciplinary courses. And we'll have in-depth interviews with a small number of students in one of those courses. I hope that this will give me different ways of getting at the same question.

Emergent Findings and Broader Significance

I'm interested in and have begun to develop a theory about what makes interdisciplinary learning work. In part, I think interdisciplinary learning works if the structure of the course builds interdisciplinary knowledge and tasks over time. That might mean starting with ideas from one discipline and then adding others later, or it might mean starting by giving a definition of interdisciplinarity and then asking students to do fairly small, well-defined tasks, building up to larger, more complex projects over the course of a term. I also think that students need to have a sense of freedom to play with ideas and ways of doing things without worrying about what will happen if they don't do it right the first time. Many of the students I interviewed told me that they enjoyed and appreciated the sense of play in the course they were taking.

> "All of these different ways of looking at things are going to add up to a richer understanding of what's going on. And this is very like my process in doing my regular research. I look at different sources and look for patterns of meaning, relationships, and so forth."

But just as important, I'm learning a lot about the process of doing this work. What's the best way to explore students' experiences in the classroom? What would you really need to know to understand this better? Should you look at an individual episode of learning, at a whole course (because interdisciplinarity is curricular as well as pedagogical), or what?

Of course one answer—an interdisciplinarian's answer—is that you need to ask the questions at various levels and in various contexts. Maybe this is why it calms me immensely to think of this as a four- or five-year project. This quarter I'm just going to get a sampling from three classes—interviews, surveys, students' papers, etc.—and that's a whole lot of data. And then in another semester, I'll go sit in on someone's class everyday. And in yet another semester I'll do something else. All of these different ways of looking at things are going to add up to a richer understanding of what's going on. And this is very like my process in doing my regular research. I look at different sources and look for patterns of meaning, relationships, and so forth. Sometimes, I feel like I'm not getting anywhere, because I'm not finding clear answers. Other times, I feel like I'm learning a lot despite the fact that I'm not finding clear answers. I'm a humanities scholar, after all. How often do I find really definitive answers on anything?

I'm also beginning to see this work in a much larger way. My image of this—thanks in part to a project that 1998 Carnegie Scholar Randy Bass is working on, the Visible Knowledge Project, which will continue and expand onto my campus as well as ten others around the country—is that my questions will become part of a collaborative project in American Studies that will continue over the next four years or so, involving faculty in various settings and contexts, coming at the questions in various ways.

Conditions for Doing the Scholarship of Teaching and Learning

The Visible Knowledge Project will help me connect this work with other scholarship on interdisciplinary learning, as I've been able to do with some of my Carnegie colleagues. But I've been lucky to have colleagues at my university who are excited about this work and eager to know what I'm finding out. Many of them have offered to help, for instance, in analyzing the data, or getting involved in some other way. In fact, every single time I have asked people at my institution to collaborate with me, they have said yes. I've had people come to me—like the folks working on the survey—with offers of help, ways they want to contribute.

In short, I've received good support locally. The timing is right, because our new general education model created an opportunity for more faculty to get involved in teaching interdisciplinary courses. Most of my colleagues and administrators are supportive. Part of this is luck; part of it is the position I'm in, in interdisciplinary studies. My job entails making connections with a lot of people from different departments, so of course that groundwork helped. People knew me, had worked with me, were willing to get involved. It's been great.

Benefits of the Work

One consequence of this work for me personally is that I'm much more aware of how things look from the students' point of view. I'm realizing at a deeper level how easy it is to assume or hope that students understand what we're doing and why—and how important it is to tell them very explicitly. This work has made me stop and think much more about how things look from the students' side of the dynamic. It's not that I've never thought about that but that I'm thinking about it now on a much deeper level. This comes especially from reading Grant Wiggins' work on backward design and also from my own research.

Another consequence—which some people might see as a downside, though I do not—is that I'm more self-conscious in my teaching, and so I'm working a lot harder on teaching. I was like a lot of people at about their tenth year of being a full-time faculty member, that is, beginning to feel kind of lazy about teaching, running the same courses over for the seventh or eighth time. My scholarship of teaching has made me see things in new ways and, because of that, I have to work much harder. And that's good.

Going through this process and the discussions with other Carnegie Scholars completely altered my attitude toward the idea of assessment. I'm still not happy with the way my university does it, by a long shot, because a lot of what we do is not useful, but I went from being one of those people who sees assessment as a stupid hoop the administration is making us go through to feeling like I now understand that some kinds of assessment questions can actually help me teach better. I hope that this will also help me figure out better ways to assess the program that I direct. I think that one of the benefits to the scholarship of teaching and learning for people who run American Studies and other interdisciplinary programs may be better approaches for assessing what your program is doing.

Lessons Learned

First, I would encourage people to stay open to various approaches, and to view the scholarship of teaching as a process of testing out different ways of looking at something. For instance, one of the best things that happened last summer is that other Carnegie Scholars warned me not to depend exclusively on ethnography but to think about other kinds of information I might need. It became clear, as we talked, that I didn't know clearly enough what I wanted to find out. It took me a while to work toward that clarity. Don't be in a rush to decide what you want to investigate and how.

A related piece of advice is to experiment with different methods and different kinds of data. It's OK to acknowledge to ourselves that we're learning a new thing, and we don't have to be experts right away. We should approach this work in a spirit of play. Mess around. See how things feel.

Finally, I'd say talk to colleagues—in your own field, and others, especially people who have done similar work. Try out your question on other people. Most of what I've learned in this I've learned from conversations with colleagues. That's a function of the kind of learner I am, but it also says something about what's useful.

REFERENCES AND RESOURCES

Wiggins, Grant, and McTighe, Jay. *Understanding by Design*. Alexandria, VA: Association for Supervision and Curriculum Development, 1998.

A Case Study of Theory, Voice, Pedagogy, and Joy

Mona Taylor Phillips
Sociology, Spelman College

Mona Phillips

Mona Phillips is associate professor of sociology at Spelman College in Atlanta, Georgia, where she teaches courses in the sociology of women, racism and culture, social psychology, sociology of the family, and general sociology. She also teaches in and serves as director of Spelman's African Diaspora and the World Program. Her students are primarily Black women of varying ethnicities, mostly traditional in age, though Mona reports that her courses also attract a few older, returning students. She recently served as co-investigator in a three-year project entitled "Survey Measures of Stress and Strain for African American Women," and as assistant director of a curriculum development project in Black Women's Studies, funded by the Ford Foundation. Her PhD is from the University of Michigan, and she attended Spelman College as an undergraduate. The interview for this case took place in February 2000.

With my project, I set out to think more precisely about the ways in which the Black women I teach can connect to their own ideas, their own process of theorizing. I wanted to investigate whether there are better ways to get them to connect their own ideas with the theories and ideas that constitute this thing we call sociological theory.

Framing the Question

I've been teaching Contemporary Sociological Theory for about five years. During that time I've become increasingly aware of the difficulty my students have in understanding theory. I don't mean particular theories or theorists, but the *concept* of theory, and what it means to theorize. There's a good deal of national attention paid to the difficulties women students face in math and science, and how those fields can be alienating for women. I saw the same thing in my students' struggle with theory, which they saw as something outside of them, something to which they had no connection. This was troubling to me because as a sociologist I see theorizing as something all of us do everyday, and as an essential part of how we make meaning from our experience.

I began to ask myself how I could make theory less alienating for my students. I started by "fooling around" with the course in ways that I thought might open up this area of learning, taking certain risks in my teaching. And then of course I wanted to know whether my efforts were succeeding and what might be lost in the process. My questions for the scholarship of teaching came out of these efforts.

My original questions have now taken an additional twist, as well. Initially my concern was with students' cognitive understanding of theory and theorizing. But I now see myself asking a question about an emotional dimension of learning—of joy, that is. I want to understand more about how I can help students see themselves as part of the wonderful process of understanding the world around them and their position in it. How do I engage them in what is after all a wonderful, joyful enterprise? I wanted to see whether or not what happens in the classroom generates that joy. And of course that means getting clearer about how I know that joy when I see it; for instance I want to test my sense that joy has a particular rhythm. And then there's the question about how I can talk about this with wider audiences in a credible and useful way, since joy is not usually among the goals and outcomes that faculty list in their syllabi.

The Context: A Course in Contemporary Sociological Theory

Contemporary Theory is the second theory course taken by Spelman sociology majors. The first, History of Social Thought, moves students through the "classical" theorists (including W.E.B. Dubois and Charles Johnson) to the sociological theorists of the 1960's and 70's. I've made a number of changes in the course in order to address the difficulty that students have with theory. One is to rethink the reading assignments in ways that add to the mix more readings by people who look like my students— African American women. This change, in turn, means moving away from the material represented in most sociological texts and introducing readings that are not really by people who are identified as sociologists but as social thinkers—like Anna Julia Cooper, a woman educator who wrote from the South in the 1890s. She critiqued the suffragist movement for its racism, the United States for its treatment of Native Americans, and African American men for their sexism and patriarchy. Scholars in women's studies use her work, which was among the first to theorize multiple identities as well as several other important ideas discussed in the discipline today. Cooper was the one who said, "I stand on a train platform, see the signs 'For Women' and 'For Colored,' and I wonder under which head I come." But to get back to the idea of introducing students to African American writers, this change also implies a shift from theory to *theorizing* and from a course in contemporary sociological thought to one in contemporary *social* thought, which is not how the course is listed. So this is a risk because I'm taking liberties with disciplinary-based content and coverage.

The other risk in these shifts is parochialism. If I build the course around readings by people of color, people who look like my students, I might gain a kind of connection for students, but I also risk imposing a parochial world. What I've done therefore in the past three years or so is to open things up in a different way and shift the lens around a little bit. We can move, for example, from Angela Davis, and her discussion of the experience of Black women, to Becky Thomson's *A Hunger So Wide and So Deep*, a book that examines eating problems among women of *varying* backgrounds and ethnicities. This shift allows the students to consider a gender issue from the perspective of women who are not like them. That is, we continue to investigate the same general topics, but we look at them from perspectives that vary from those of most of the students.

Another example of shifting the lens is my use of Omi and Winant's *Racial Formation in the United States*. Both of the authors are male, and neither one is African American, but they are talking about race in a useful way because they're talking about race as a political construction in the latter half of the twentieth century. It's a very theoretical work. It's actually a piece that doesn't center the discussion about race around African Americans. Clearly African Americans are part of the discussion, but the authors also talk about how many groups get racialized. That's what I mean when I say we broaden the discussion. We're talking about race as an ongoing political construction that happens in response to other political movements. Thus we get to talk about the far right and the conservative right and all of their different components as responses to the women's movement and the civil rights movement. But it's not just about African Americans.

> "I would describe my method as triangulated—bringing together evidence from several different sources and methods. But with any of them, I apply the principle that you have to be careful about the conclusions you draw."

As a result I am working to free myself from constraints of two different kinds. One comes from the very particular circumstances of teaching in an historically Black college, and the double consciousness that entails—the sense of preparing these women to go out into a world that may from the very beginning doubt them—because they didn't go to Stanford, they went to Spelman. This is a very old idea about African American education—that you overprepare; you make sure that the students know what other people know and *more*. I had to free myself from that, and that was the hardest thing.

I've also had to free myself from the strength of the discipline, but that has been less difficult because I've had help from colleagues in various settings, most notably from Black women's studies, including the work of Beverly Guy-Sheftall on this campus. Also, here at Spelman, I'm involved in a course on the African diaspora in the world, which is multi- and interdisciplinary. As part of my involvement with this course I have had to talk with people outside my field. That's been a precious experience because it's helped me to think of things in a broader way and be willing to break out of the boundaries of my discipline.

Gathering the Evidence

I would describe my method as triangulated—bringing together evidence from several different sources and methods. But with any of them, I apply the principle that you have to be careful about the conclusions you draw.

One strategy involves what I call "the ideas assignment," in which I ask the students to use their sociological imaginations in the examination of their own ideas—not to talk about the sociological imagination that *sociologists* have, but to look at the extent to which the ways they themselves think and theorize, and their own perspectives, are partly a function of their times. The assignment asks them to define their times, to be self-conscious of what it means to be born and grow up in these times. I ask them to situate their work—and I always refer to their research as their work—in these times. We can do it very nicely with Dubois and with Marx, but what about the students' contemporary influences? The students tell me this is a difficult assignment; part of the difficulty stems from the fact that I have them work in groups. Not only do they have to define their times as individuals, they have to arrive at a consensus about what constitutes their times. But they always come up with incredible work. And it's a first step to get students to take ownership of their ideas.

"A principle behind my choice of methods is the same principle that guides much of my scholarship—respect for the voices of the participants, in this case the students."

I intended to use this assignment twice, as a pre- and post-test, but I couldn't do that last semester because, perceiving that need to overprepare African American women for a hostile world, I ran out of time. In the future I will make sure there's time for students to go back to their initial assignment and write about how they would now do it differently. Because I'm looking for change or development over the course of the semester, rather than mastery, this "post-test" reflection will not be graded. I should also say that this business of pre- and post- is tricky. My students are taking other sociology courses concurrently with mine. And they're living in the world, learning things from their experiences. So I *am* interested in their reflecting back on the assignment, and thinking about how they would do it differently, but I won't be able to infer that the differences they identify are wholly a function of this course. I can't draw that conclusion. In fact, I want to ask students to *tell me*, if they can, what influenced their later perspective, to try to tease out the various influences.

Another area of evidence is the actual writing the students do. I began looking at student work more closely, looking for indicators of ownership. I look for a comfort and ease and grasp of what they've read. I ask, Are they talking back to what they've read? Are they in conversation with it? Or are they instead merely saying to me, "This person said this"? That's not a good sign. I want to recognize the student in the middle of the paper; if I can recognize her, then there is ownership, and that indicates deep learning.

Another strategy I'm using this spring is focus groups comprised of students (about eight per group) who took the course last semester. The focus group will ask about the relationship of the course to what the students are currently doing within the departmentally required individual research project. So I'll ask them about the ideas assignment and how they would do it differently now. I'll ask, for instance, What was it in the course that helped them either to clarify their times or to clarify their ideas in relation to the times? What in the course did they not find helpful? What might they find more helpful in developing their ideas and voices as social theorists?

The other piece of the focus groups is to ask students to describe a moment when they felt joy in their own ideas. I'm not defining joy for them; their answers will define it. I know what it feels like to me, and I think I know when I see it in the classroom, but the point of the focus group discussion is to hear from students what it feels like to them. So the focus group will help with this. It's an occasion for the students to "go meta."

In fact, I really like this idea of "going meta," which appears in the piece on the scholarship of teaching by Pat Hutchings and Lee Shulman in *Change* magazine. The focus group is an occasion for all of us—my students and me—to go meta. That's one of the reasons (and I had to really think about this) I would not have someone else run the focus group, though I know that's often the preferred model. I am not, frankly, concerned about "contaminating" the discussion through my presence. The point of the focus group is a reflection upon and re-articulation of an experience we—my students and I—have had together. It's appropriate to undertake this as a group. In her book *Talking Back*, Patricia Hill Collins discusses dialogue as a valid knowledge process—a kind of call and response. That's how I see the focus group.

A principle behind my choice of methods is the same principle that guides much of my scholarship—respect for the voices of the participants, in this case the students. Often times when you impose a method, you impose a voice. You have it all plotted out and planned in the beginning. I'm trying to strike a balance between rigor and flexibility. This work has to unfold and take shape as the course itself, as well as the students' experience, unfolds and takes shape. That's the theoretical position that shapes my work.

My decisions about how to conduct this investigation are also a function of the type of questions I'm asking, which are not "bottom line" questions. I'm not trying to prove anything or show that one classroom approach is by definition better than another. I'm trying to describe as fully as I can a new way of thinking of my field and what it means to teach in keeping with that transformed view.

I'm aware that there are people who will look at my methods and argue that this work lacks rigor. Rigor, for many, entails numbers, quantitative data. One of the tasks for the scholarship of teaching and learning is to rethink what constitutes rigor, drawing on fields beyond the sciences. For instance, I would claim that rigor involves careful examination of the appropriateness of *whatever* method is chosen. Rigor involves considering context, goals, and purposes before deciding on method. So I'm asking for a harder kind of rigor, which is to start from the question and context. And I'm talking about a right match between methods and core values. Many of my choices about how to do this work stem from a commitment to hearing others' voices, making them authentic participants and collaborators in the investigation.

Benefits of the Work

At the most basic level, a benefit to the scholarship of teaching is that it puts a name on something that's an important part of the work of faculty in teaching institutions. Naming is a way of valuing.

Secondly, I value the work I've been doing because as a scholar I want to make sense of things. More specifically, I want to explore these questions because I care about my students' capacity to go forth with confidence. I'm interested in understanding what happens in a course in which this sense of confidence and joy is not just a by-product but a deliberate intention, a central and explicit goal. Too often we treat our most important goals as hoped-for by-products rather than as core principles that shape the course.

Finally, there's the benefit that the process of investigating the course, and being explicit about the fact that I'm doing that, has made my students more conscious of their learning and growth; I'm going meta and so are they. As I wrote in one of my progress reports to the Carnegie Scholars, doing the scholarship of teaching and learning changed the power dynamic in my course. Students feel more free to tell me if something isn't working. And they're much more active in shaping the course.

For instance, one student told me that a book I was using later in the semester would be better at the beginning. Another told me that I needed to be more explicit at the beginning of the semester about the fact that I'm using a feminist perspective in designing and teaching the course; when students stumble into this realization, she told me, they find it alienating and problematic. Those are suggestions I can use to further develop the course.

Another example arose recently: A student said it would be useful if, at the end of the class session, I summarized the important points. It's not clear what we're supposed to get from the discussion, she said. This was actually an interesting exchange because it got us into a discussion about the purpose of discussion. I told the class that I would not want to summarize at the end of the hour because that would put a period at the end—talking about race is complex, and a neat summary statement would be untrue to that complexity. So we decided that it would be useful instead to start the next class with questions that tie back to points from the previous discussion.

Conditions for Doing the Scholarship of Teaching and Learning

One general circumstance has helped me: My institution sees work on teaching as central to our institutional identity, and in a very public way. More specifically, it has been very helpful to have a chair who values and supports this kind of work as well as colleagues who are interested in it. The course I've been examining is integral to our departmental curriculum, and there's an interest in how my work might affect other parts of the program. For instance, the faculty member directing students' theses has noted an improvement in their work, so we're talking about the connection between my course and the larger curriculum. I keep my colleagues informed about what I'm doing by sending around periodic updates and documents.

Lessons Learned

First, I'd say be patient with yourself. It helped me a lot to do my work with some leisure, not to be in a hurry to come up with "findings." Teaching and learning involve complex and complicated dynamics; it's unreasonable to expect quick, neat answers. The work needs to develop and take shape over time. Second, be prepared to discover that the work raises more questions than it answers. This is good because the fact is that we don't really know much about what goes on in classrooms.

REFERENCES AND RESOURCES

Collins, Patricia Hill. *Black Feminist Thought: Knowledge, Consciousness, and the Politics of Empowerment.* Boston: Unwin Hyman, 1990.

Hutchings, Pat, and Shulman, Lee S. "The Scholarship of Teaching: New Elaborations, New Developments. *Change* 31, 5 (1999): 11–15.

Omi, Michael, and Howard Winant. *Racial Formation in the United States: From the 1960s to the 1980s.* New York: Routledge & Kegan Paul, 1986.

Thomson, Becky W. *A Hunger So Wide and So Deep: American Women Speak Out on Eating Problems.* Minneapolis: University of Minnesota Press, 1994.

CASE STUDY

Mariolina Rizzi Salvatori
English, University of Pittsburgh

Mariolina Salvatori

Mariolina Rizzi Salvatori is associate professor of English at the University of Pittsburgh, a research university with an enrollment of about 30,000 students. Mariolina holds a doctorate in "Lingue, Letterature ed Istituzioni dell'Europa Occidentale" (Sezione Germanica) from the Istituto Universitario Orientale (Naples, Italy). In 1976, she earned a PhD in comparative literature from the University of Pittsburgh. In 1981, she was hired by the University of Pittsburgh as assistant professor of English with teaching responsibilities both in the literature and composition programs. Since then, her goal has been to argue, in theory and practice, for approaches that problematize the institutional and intellectual divisions between the two disciplines, at the undergraduate and graduate level.

Mariolina has been deeply involved with the teaching of teaching in her department, as director of the Committee for the Evaluation and Advancement of Teaching (CEAT), and as teacher of the Teaching of Composition Seminar. CEAT and Seminar are designed to provide theoretical, instructional, and practical support for first-year TAs/TFs whose reappointment is contingent on their satisfactory performance in these two contexts. Mariolina's scholarship on the interconnectedness of reading and writing and her "pedagogy of difficulty" have influenced several curricular reforms in her department and have helped graduate students and faculty within her department and elsewhere to reshape and refine their scholarship of teaching. The interview for this case study took place in May 2000.

My investigation focuses on the role of difficulty in the learning process. What counts as difficulty, and how do learners experience it? What forms does it take? Is difficulty a constitutive part of learning? Is there a relationship between difficulty and educational approaches? How do teachers teach students to deal with difficulty? These are important questions for me because the premise of my scholarship of teaching and learning is that "moments of difficulty" often contain the seeds of understanding. In her essay "The Difficulty of Reading," Helen Reguerio Elam argues that American education does not take well to the idea of difficulty. She suggests that our penchant for easy and immediate solutions leads us to expect and demand in all areas of life—including reading—an ease of achievement that is antithetical to the complexities of our thinking process. I agree with Elam, but I want to complicate what she says. I want to suggest that in American education concepts of and approaches to difficulties function as a sort of "Great Divide." On one side of it, the site of "novice and reluctant learners," difficulties are complications that are not profitable, or economically viable, for them to identify, to address, let alone to resolve. As Elam says, they go against the grain of educational efficiency. On the other side of the divide, the site of "consummate and passionate learners," difficulties and the ability to understand, process, and live with them are a marker of learners' high culture, sophistication, and intelligence. This side nurtures a culture and a cult of difficulty. On this side, the language and concepts developed to handle difficulties and to keep them in circulation are esoteric, extremely specialized, and exclusionary. I am interested in exploring the reasons for this cultural divide, and the consequences. I want to frame "moments of difficulty" as examples of incipient scholarship for novice learners as well. Specifically, I want to write about and theorize the often-startling production, exchange, and revision of knowledge that a focus on difficulty can foster, both for teachers and students.

Framing the Question

My goal is to investigate the work that students, undergraduate and graduate, advanced and remedial, do with demanding texts as a way of learning more and possibly revising what we know about the act of reading. I want to examine the kind of reading and writing they produce when they encounter difficult texts. I want to uncover their unarticulated assumptions about what they think it means to read and to write. I want to study the extent to which what they leave unarticulated, and so unexaminable, affects their performance. My purpose is to develop this idea in ways that can move all students to deeper forms of understanding.

My interest in difficulty grows out of personal experiences and needs. When I left Italy, I had completed my university education there. As a foreign graduate student in this country, in an educational context whose conventions I didn't know, I found myself experiencing many moments of difficulty, which in retrospect I have come to see as moments of understanding on my part—that is, as moments in which I was understanding *differently*. Occasionally, I would be disoriented by a question one of my teachers asked. I could not figure out why the question was being asked in that particular way, or why it would be asked at all. And yet, I noticed it seemed to make sense to everybody else. My tendency, at first, was to mask my disorientation, to pretend it was not there, to learn to do things as others were doing. But later, as I gained more confidence in myself and in what I knew, I understood that the questions were perceived by me as difficult, or puzzling, because they reflected a set of cultural assumptions and educational approaches that were foreign to me. And I realized that by making visible *my* cultural assumptions, and those of my teachers and classmates, I could better understand and put pressure on what made me experience some questions as disorienting. By engaging rather than suppressing difficulties, I began to turn what could have been impediments to learning into a source of and motivation for learning. That's when I began to think of myself as not inadequate. Interestingly, I then started noticing similar moments in my classroom. I noticed that sometimes I was unintentionally doing to my students what my teachers had unintentionally done to me. I tried to freeze those classroom moments and look at them carefully.

One of the most fundamental lessons I learned was the productive pressure that classroom work puts on the theory-practice relationship, both in terms of practice as the rigorous enactment of theory, and of practice as the testing ground of theory. I loved and respected teaching (I come from a long lineage of teachers) and took my preparations quite seriously. But my love and respect for teaching and my assiduous preparations were not enough for me to be a good teacher. I soon discovered that I needed to know more about how to teach, *and* how to teach differently. Fortunately, at the beginning of my experience as a TA in the English Department (I had been teaching undergraduate and graduate courses in Italian until then), I took a required Seminar in Teaching Literature, which was team-taught by Robert Marshall and Dan Tannacito. Then at the start of my career as an assistant professor, I audited the Seminar in Teaching Composition, taught by William E. Coles. These three teachers/scholars had an indelible influence on me. They fueled my love for teaching and for the teaching of teaching; they taught me to reflect on and ask critical questions of my own teacherly assumptions, proclivities, and decisions.

Another teacher affected my theory of teaching less directly, but even more pervasively. Her name is Marcia Landy. I was her graduate assistant in several "difficult" courses: Twentieth-Century Comparative Literature, film courses, and women's studies courses. As much as she could responsibly do it, she treated me as an equal. She gave me a few overt suggestions. Mostly she taught me how to teach by assuming that I could and that I knew how to do it. But she was ready to intervene and help me, when I needed it. It was terrifying but exhilarating. I watched her in action and studied the effects of what she did on her students. I was wise enough to know I could and should not duplicate all of her moves because of our theoretical and temperamental differences (this is a lesson that I would like to pass on). So I watched, and studied, and translated her moves until they worked for me.

From Dr. Landy, I learned to pose tough questions for my students, questions that were meant to lead them to a theoretical understanding of reading that I thought was important. But at first I asked these questions without making clear to my students *why* I was asking them, or what context or assumptions led me to ask them. I put them on a propitious path, but I blindfolded them on the way to that path. I began to notice that when I asked these difficult, reflexive questions, many of my students moved farthest away from me—they could not cooperate, or they entered the dialogue almost like automatons, speaking things that they didn't really understand but thought I wanted to hear. Paying attention to my students' difficulties became a constant focus in my teaching, at both the undergraduate and graduate levels. But it was in the context of teaching composition that I began to see the real usefulness of paying attention to students' moments of difficulty.

I need to stress that my interest in difficulty is also intimately connected with my theoretical background in the discipline. That is, my own approach to reading and to the interpretation of texts is very much shaped by the work I do with phenomenology and hermeneutics, reader-response and reception theory, as well as theories of literacy. As a result, the questions I ask as a teacher are the distillation, in a way, of my understanding of reading as a process involving difficult moments, which I see not as signs of inadequacy on the reader's part, but rather as signs that the reader has sensed and/or identified a textual difficulty that she needs to capture and engage, interpret and respond to.

My work, then, has an additional, but indirect, goal: I believe teachers *should* ask questions about their students' work that grow out of their theoretical background; they should read and engage their students' texts by asking of them the same kinds of questions they ask of the scholarly texts they read and write. In addition, they should question the theories they espouse in terms of how they affect and reflect their students' learning. These are, for me, ways of nurturing and disseminating the scholarship of teaching and learning.

The Context: English Studies and Composition

Composition is a required course on my campus, which means that in freshman composition courses I see students from many different disciplines. What's also true is that they come to the course with different sets of assumptions, which means that any one question I might ask will pose different kinds of difficulties for my diverse students. Out of this circumstance grew the genesis of what I now call "the difficulty paper," a heuristic that enables me and my students to capture some of those difficulties, and to turn them into moments of understanding.

Why do I pay so much attention to difficulty? I want to disabuse students from believing that difficulties are always and necessarily signs of incompetence, inadequacy. I want them to learn to recognize difficulties as signs of a kind of thinking that stops before coming to fruition. Students, in this educational system, are seldom taught or encouraged to tackle difficulties on their own. Under the guise of "modeling," often teachers solve those difficulties for them, in front of them, without necessarily making visible the crucial decisions and moves they made. And most textbooks reduce the complexity of learning to sequences of easy steps. These are ways of condemning the intelligence of students, of deciding a priori that something is too difficult for them, that it exceeds their ability to understand.

I know, of course, that to work closely with students, finding out what they know and don't know how to do so as to begin the investigation there, takes time, and requires a different training than the one usually given to teachers. But if we are really interested in promoting deep understanding for all students, rather than for a privileged few, we need to reconsider how we prepare college and university teachers to teach.

I didn't come to this understanding all at once, of course. I know, in retrospect, that I stumbled upon it by accident, not fully recognizing at first what stood in my way. I remember, as a beginning instructor, feeling impatient with students who would find the texts I chose difficult. I knew I chose demanding texts, but even so I found it frustrating when they would declare, "This text is too difficult for me" or "It does not make any sense," pinning, I thought, the responsibility of making things understandable on the text rather than on themselves. In order to keep myself calm in the face of this frustration, I began asking these students to give me a list of all the things they found difficult in the text, and I used the blackboard to enumerate all the difficulties they identified. I used this strategy, really, to create a pause, during which I could think of appropriate questions to ask.

And then I began to realize, as I was writing those difficult elements on the board, that my students were giving me, potentially, an interpretation of the text. But they didn't know that. In other words, the elements they identified as difficulties were *in fact* difficult. And for good reasons. Students were "bumping into" linguistic, structural, or factual elements that a reader must engage in order to come to an understanding of the text. They were coming up against a kind of door in the text (to borrow the metaphor Mills Kelly has used when he has talked to me about how, in his teaching, he focuses on difficulty); they saw it was there, but they didn't see how to open it. I wanted my students to learn to open that door by themselves. For them to do that, they needed to learn to see that their difficulties were not a sign of inadequacy but markers of a particular kind of understanding, reflecting a set of assumptions that might have been inadequate to the present task, or misplaced. (This is where Bill Cerbin's path and mine converge, I think.) By bringing attention to this dynamic, I noticed, and they noticed, their skills and the pleasure they took taking ownership of those skills. Out of this experience came what I call the "difficulty paper assignment," which now I use in every course I teach for undergraduates and graduates.

> "I believe teachers *should* ask questions about their students' work that grow out of their theoretical background; they should read and engage their students' texts by asking of them the same kinds of questions they ask of the scholarly texts they read and write."

I continue to wrestle with the question of what kinds of knowledge and understanding make it possible to identify difficulties. How do we name this understanding? Or is it a knowledge without the knower's understanding that it is knowledge? Maybe it does represent a step toward, though perhaps not yet full, understanding. I keep going back to Gadamer and Polanyi to deepen this investigation and to ride it forward.

Gathering the Evidence: The Difficulty Paper

The difficulty paper is a simple, yet as I am finding out, very powerful, assignment; it asks students to identify something difficult in a text and describe, in detail, why they experience it as difficult. More often than not, out of the description comes an act of interpretation and understanding. It's difficult for the teacher who sees the turn toward interpretation before her student does to resist saying, "See, what you are really saying is …" But it is important that the teacher learn to ask questions that make it possible for the student to come to the realization.

I want to make clear that, in my approach, the difficulty paper is a preliminary kind of work. It does not at once, nor the first time, "open the door." When I teach, be it literature or composition or theory, at the undergraduate or graduate level, I assign a difficulty paper for each new reading. Students are supposed to hand in a one-or-two-page typed account of a particular difficulty or moment of disorientation (sometimes I vary the language) they have encountered reading a particular poem, or essay, or short story, or theoretical text. They hand in the paper *before* we discuss the work, so they don't know at that moment what the other students in the classroom are experiencing as difficult. Usually, two or three patterns of difficulties emerge from these papers. These patterns can be roughly categorized as (specialized) language, gender, race, culture, genre, and theoretical difficulties. I regularly select two or three common difficulties for class discussion. The purpose of the discussion is both to validate the difficulties and to uncover the sets of assumptions that prevent students from seeing them as generative of meaning. Sometimes around the fourth or fifth week of the semester I abandon the difficulty paper because the students have so much internalized the process that they don't need the heuristic anymore. They now look *for* rather than away from difficulties. They wrestle with them, and in so doing, they come to interesting conclusions about the who and what and how of making meaning. I don't grade the difficulty papers but they must be turned in or there is a penalty. The grade goes to the essay that results from the difficulty paper process, which I'll talk about later in this report.

The difficulty paper serves several functions. For me, its most basic function is to teach students how to identify specific difficulties and not move away from them. But it also serves another function. When a student makes his or her difficulty public, she demonstrates a level of trust and performs an act of responsibility that demand equal trust and responsibility from her teacher and classmates. That trust should not be violated. Carefully monitored class discussions should teach students to respectfully analyze the difficulty under investigation, to hypothesize reasons for it, and to map out plans to come to terms with it. This approach teaches students to think of the processes of interpretation as public, visible, and collaborative. And in the process, students learn that when they identify their difficulties, they are not punished for them, nor are they left stranded with them.

Here is a possible scenario. Imagine an undergraduate class in literature or composition. A student is reading a poem and one of his assumptions is that a poem is a kind of narrative, a plausible assumption for some poems but not for every poem. Let's assume that at first this assumption works well, but when the poem takes a turn away from narrative, the student bumps up against a difficulty. Thinking along and through a narrative line no longer works. Narration halts. Suddenly the poem stops making sense within the established pattern. What has happened is that the student has (correctly) perceived a turn in the form of the poem, but does not know how to go down the unexpected path the change points toward. The student labels that moment as a difficult moment, a roadblock. This is, then, an opportunity to invite students to imagine why the poem might take this turn. All of a sudden, the classroom becomes abuzz with hypotheses: Maybe the poet didn't know what else to do, or maybe the turn from the narrative line of the poem is intentional on the poet's part. Maybe the poet is giving a clue. Maybe the poet is telling the reader something about poetry, or narration. Why might the poet do that? What effect does it create? What else could happen at that point? What if? Then what? These are questions that students can engage, questions that appropriately reframed can make them discern what's behind the text's difficulty, or their difficulty with it. Difficulties become something out of which they can learn to make sense. This is where interpretation begins and unfolds.

Recently, I have begun to ask students to write a difficulty paper on the course description. I don't know whether this happens in other disciplines but in undergraduate English classes, some students do not even read the course description. At the end of the term, some of them do not even remember their instructor's name. The difficulty paper on the course description forces them to read it, and to become aware of and come to terms with the course's requirements. So it has a very practical function. But the assignment proves useful in another way: It sets up a context conducive to uncovering and making explicit the different assumptions students bring to education, and to the course in particular—and how those assumptions match or do not match those of the teacher. I often move into this discussion by first tackling the instructor's name question/difficulty, and, in my case, the non-native flag it carries. Many years of experience have taught me to reframe what can be outrageously offensive comments into questions that problematize common assumptions about who gets to teach which subject and why. If the alien status question does not come up, or does not seem to be an issue, the omnipresent and seemingly bland difficulty of not "remembering the instructor's name" can be usefully harnessed to raise crucial questions like: What does it mean not to try to remember one's instructor's name? Who is that nameless person in the classroom? What's her function? Can "not remembering" be an attempt to take authority away from her? To what extent does this "not remembering" reflect and reproduce a depersonalized and depersonalizing construction of education? These questions open a door into a field of inquiry worth investigating.

> "This approach teaches students to think of the processes of interpretation as public, visible, and collaborative. And in the process, students learn that when they identify their difficulties, they are not punished for them, nor are they left stranded with them."

But the difficulty paper on the course description allows for discussion of another important topic: prerequisite knowledge and prior understanding. For example, my approach is shaped by my interpretive and hermeneutical proclivities, by my interest in how readers construct meanings. Students who come to my courses with an historical perspective, and a background in literary history, might not have a clue how to answer, or even to ask, a question framed by reader-response, or by reception theories. I need to know what perspectives and assumptions students bring to the course, and I need to clarify for my students why I am doing what I'm doing. (This much I have taught myself.) This is a kind of back-pedaling that I don't think we do enough of. Or at least, I didn't at first. I often walked into the classroom assuming that the students were already with me. But they were not, of course. By not paying attention to what they/I didn't know and need to know about each other, I wasted a lot of precious time.

The difficulty paper assignment also functions as a protection against plagiarism. In my department we teach multiple sections of composition, many of which are taught by graduate assistants, all working from the same syllabus (and enrolled in a seminar on teaching at the same time). One consequence of the shared syllabus is that there is a tremendous possibility that students will plagiarize each other's papers. This is not the kind of collective inquiry I am after. Students live together in the dorms, and they get the same assignments; for some of them, it's almost, one might say, an invitation to plagiarize. But the difficulty paper circumvents this temptation. Because students cannot turn in work that does not grow out of an initial difficulty paper, it is nearly impossible for them to borrow a paper from someone else. Their writing must stem from personal "difficulty" with the text.

As will be clear here, I hope, the difficulty paper serves a number of useful functions. Most relevant to my study as a Carnegie Scholar, however, is that it provides my primary window into the process whereby moments of difficulty can be transformed into occasions for learning. Much of my work consists of using and carefully examining the difficulty papers my students produce in order to learn how that process leads to growth in understanding on subsequent tasks. That is, I'm studying how what they learn about surmounting a given difficulty might enable them to work through subsequent and different difficulties.

Recently I have been gathering evidence by working in partnership with faculty in several other fields. This phase of my study is very much shaped by questions, specifically skeptical questions, posed to me by my fellow Carnegie Scholars. In particular, John Eby, a sociologist, asked me whether my focus on difficulty might be taken by my students as a way of saying, "It's OK to have difficulties." Yes it might, and it should, given my theory of difficulty. But to say that is not to say that either the students' job or my job is done. I go on to guide students in their search for ways of unpacking those difficulties. And later I expect them to show me how they can initiate this process on their own. Ted Wagenaar, also a sociologist, raised the possibility that the productiveness of this approach might be highly idiosyncratic. He acknowledges that it works for me, but, he asks, what reason do I have to believe that it would be powerful in other settings, used by other teachers? That is a good research question, actually, because it challenges the researcher to consider the broader implications of her project.

Ted's and John's questions have pushed me to enlarge my investigation, and to gather evidence beyond my own classroom, which is one of the hallmarks of the scholarship of teaching and learning. Toward this end, I have arranged to have a number of faculty adapt the difficulty assignment to their context and then share their students' papers with me. Mills Kelly, a Carnegie Scholar in history at Texas Tech, is one of these; the others (not Carnegie Scholars) are from composition, theatre arts, cultural studies, and creative writing. I would like to make a similar arrangement with faculty in math or chemistry as well. My hunch is that the exploration of difficulties can be even more powerful there than in the humanities because it would force students to articulate their thinking more carefully, which is a strategy that is now regaining ground in the sciences.

Looking at the practice of other teachers, in other fields, will, I hope, give me a clearer sense of whether indeed this approach is idiosyncratic. Inevitably, I believe, there will always be an element of this in any teacher's performance insofar as fruitful teaching strategies should grow out of and reflect the theoretical proclivities of the individual teacher. But at the same time, they should also be somewhat generalizable and explainable, though not entirely portable. I am trying to uncover whether the focus on difficulty is something that will benefit other faculty—not the difficulty paper per se but the part difficulty plays in the learning process.

Emergent Findings and Broader Significance

What can I say at this point about the effect of the difficulty papers on students' understanding in my classes? I can say, first, that I identify impact by looking for "markers" in students' writing that indicate movement toward more complicated forms of thinking.

At the undergraduate level, one marker is a more complex sentence structure. I look for students to move away from the "statement model" of writing—one declarative sentence after another, unconnected—toward a style in which sentences connect, sometimes by opposition to one another, sometimes by reflective comments. I look for sentences that articulate thinking, in progress, rather than those that ventriloquize received wisdom. I look for sentences that use markers such as "but" and "on the other hand." Those are, at the minimum, moments when students begin to complicate what they say as they say it. To use "but" is to imply that there is another possibility to consider. "I say this because" marks a moment of reflection, of accountability. Obviously, some students know how to use these linguistic features mechanically. It's not their sheer presence I look for, but whether or not they function as signposts for deeper understanding.

Another marker is students' ability to pose questions that are open-ended rather than rhetorical (by which I mean a question that already has a given answer). I look for questions that are risky to ask because they do not lead to clear-cut answers, or easy solutions. I look for questions that posit unforeseen possibilities. I also look for moments when, as they write, students seem to become aware of themselves thinking, and begin to reflect on the interpretations they have made, the steps they have taken, or are taking, or could have taken. These are really very interesting moments, because the writing does not read like the work of an automaton. It is writing produced by a mind that thinks and that draws its readers to think along, or in opposition.

Looking at these markers, I can say that most students in my classes do make progress toward more complex forms of thinking—though not all of them to an equal degree. But I must say that this work aims not to prove that this particular strategy will lead to a particular outcome. The processes I'm interested in are not neatly measurable. My real interest lies in providing a way of thinking about difficulties that can help explain and enhance the experience of students. Let me stress that when I illustrate this particular strategy of mine, which does not stand for my whole approach to teaching, I am not trying to offer a quick fix, to swap a recipe. I am trying instead to suggest that strategies should be the distillation of a teacher's theory of learning. And, to return to Ted's question, let me say, finally, that this approach works for me and for teachers interested in tapping the thinking and reflexive processes of their students; but it would not work for all faculty. For example, it would be counterproductive for a teacher who is not interested in having students ask questions about the foundational concepts and practices of the discipline, or for a teacher whose goals are to have students know certain key facts and events rather than explore the ways writers think and write or researchers identify and select key facts and events. In other words, the difficulty paper works for approaches to teaching that are highly reflexive.

At the graduate level, it is tremendously productive to uncover moments of difficulty as markers of inchoate interdisciplinarity, for example the different theoretical constructions of individual or individualism, of creativity and inspiration, or writing and reading, that make it almost impossible for a creative writer to understand the critique of those concepts articulated by a practicing Marxist critic. And vice versa. At the graduate level, moments of difficulty can function as challenges to students to learn to talk across programmatic and disciplinary lines.

Conditions for Doing the Scholarship of Teaching and Learning

If I had not been at the University of Pittsburgh, with the colleagues I have here, I might have glossed over this issue of difficulty. I might have never seen it as an arena for scholarly exploration and research. It might, that is, have been important to *me*, but I might not have had the opportunity to talk to other people about it, and therefore the courage to publish about it. I might have been able to make it a central issue of my teaching but not bring it to the work of other teachers.

I say *courage* because in fact this work runs counter to the ways most faculty think of teaching and learning. Some, for instance, might (do?) look at what I do and claim that my focus on difficulty makes me ipso facto a remedial teacher, and that teaching remediation is not intellectually challenging. It's boring. Anybody can do it. Or they might say that my approach, much like the work of textbooks I am critical of, explains away difficulty. These would be troubling misreadings of what I do and of the work I argue every teacher should do. Even before I became involved with the Carnegie Foundation—and the work it promotes and sustains—I had thought of and argued for teaching as the interconnection and reciprocal monitoring of theory and practice, as the epitome of intellectual activity (my name for this is "pedagogy as reflexive praxis") (Salvatori, *Pedagogy*). I was already thinking of teaching as the testing ground for a teacher's deep understanding. I believe that if I know something but I don't know how to teach it, I don't really know and understand it deeply. If I cannot teach what I know, I need to reflect further on and investigate what and how I know. This is a tough realization to achieve. Teaching in ways that don't prevent students from coming to their own conclusions, teaching in ways that invite a teacher's self-reflection, is demanding. It can be risky. If the foundational concepts and assumptions of my discipline are of little help to my students, if they do not account for and in fact do violence to their experiences, then that's an opportune time for me to reconsider how my discipline constructs, assembles, and distributes knowledge.

It should be evident from my musings that my work is and has not necessarily been an easy match with dominant views of scholarship, views shaped by the assumptions that to know subject matter well, and to love it, are adequate preparation to teach others to understand and love it as well. This kind of knowing and loving may contribute to but do not insure the kind of teaching that the scholarship of teaching and learning argues for. What I am saying is that I couldn't have done this work in a department that doesn't value teaching as mine does. The present chair, and the previous ones, have made it clear that good, responsible teaching is expected and respected. At tenure time, faculty deliberations take into consideration the candidate's teaching record and philosophy of teaching. Even if not everyone in the department shares this view completely, there has always been enough of a critical mass for me to have interlocutors, for me to talk with people—to have colleagues I can trust, an intellectual community.

The support of one's dean is very important as well. If the dean claims to value teaching, then of course that statement makes certain things possible. But the commitment must be more than just verbal. While colleagues can sustain and energize one's commitment to the scholarship of teaching and learning, it is the institution that can make the difference for how culture at large, academic and non-academic, values and respects this kind of intellectual work. Research universities can do this by granting faculty time off from committee work (rather than from teaching) as well as by awarding them money, public recognition, and respect.

I have been able to make the scholarship of teaching central to my career. But I must also admit that I began focusing more on this kind of work after tenure. Could I have done it before? Probably not as openly. At the time I began raising questions about pedagogy, the mere mention of "pedagogy" was problematic; the term and the topic carried heavy negative connotations in the humanities. In this sense, my book (published after I had tenure) *Pedagogy: Disturbing History, 1819–1929* was an attempt to get at where those negative connotations come from, historically. It represented, if you will, an answer to a difficulty I was confronting. It grew out of my own difficulty paper. That was fifteen years ago. Things have changed. But much more needs to be done along the lines proposed by the Carnegie Foundation.

> "It should be evident from my musings that my work is and has not necessarily been an easy match with dominant views of scholarship, views shaped by the assumptions that to know subject matter well, and to love it, are adequate preparation to teach others to understand and love it as well."

Lessons Learned

There are ways of doing one's scholarship and using the classroom as the testing ground for that scholarship. Institutions should encourage young faculty to acknowledge and remedy the fact that what the culture at large sees as "scholarship" does not necessarily include what we mean by the scholarship of teaching and learning. Institutions should make it possible for young faculty to learn to do in the classroom what they have learned and have been expected to do in the "scholarly" publications that earn them tenure. And young faculty need to learn to articulate in their own terms to other faculty and administrators what they are doing in their classroom. They need to disabuse skeptical or misinformed administrators of assuming that teaching is an off-the-cuff, improvisational activity that can provide a refuge from "real scholarship." This view of teaching devalues teachers, students, scholarship, and institutions.

Let me end with two specific and direct suggestions gleaned from my own reflections on my teaching: First, don't try to imitate the "model teachers" you admire. Study what they do, but translate what they do into strategies that work for you, strategies that are extensions and representations of your theoretical framework. Look closely at what you know, at the knowledge that is the subject matter of your scholarly work and write an assignment, or a sequence of assignments, that distill, in the instructions they give, the steps necessary to think in the rich and complicated ways that make you the kind of scholar you are. If you want your students to think the ways historians, hermeneuticists, biologists, or attorneys do, create assignments or classroom discussions that make it possible for them to make those moves, to understand them, and to reflect on their effects.

Secondly, think as a teacher of teachers. Add this "meta" level to your reflections on teaching: It puts pressure on some confusing moves we rely on, on blurry assumptions. And it makes visible, sharable, and teachable what has become invisible to us because it is so habitual.

REFERENCES AND RESOURCES

Bruner, Jerome. *Actual Minds, Possible Worlds.* Cambridge: Harvard UP, 1986.

Elam, Helen Reguerio. "The Difficulty of Reading." *The Idea of Difficulty in Literature.* Ed. Alan C. Purves. New York: SUNY, 1991.

Gadamer, Hans-Georg. *Reason in the Age of Science.* Trans. Frederick G. Lawrence. Cambridge, Massachusetts: MIT P, 1996.

Gadamer, Hans-Georg. *Philosophical Hermeneutics.* Trans. and ed. David E. Linge. Berkeley: U of California P, 1976.

Gadamer, Hans-Georg. *Truth and Method.* New York: Continuum, 1975.

Glassick, Charles E., Mary Taylor Huber, Gene I. Maeroff. *Scholarship Assessed: Evaluation of the Professoriate.* San Francisco: Jossey-Bass Publishers, 1997.

Iser, Wolfgang. *The Act of Reading.* Baltimore: Johns Hopkins UP, 1978.

Kermode, Frank. *The Genesis of Secrecy.* Cambridge: Harvard UP, 1979.

Newkirk, Thomas. "Looking for Trouble: A Way to Unmask Our Readings." *College English* 46 (1984): 756–766.

Polanyi, Michael. *Personal Knowledge: Toward a Post-Critical Philosophy.* Chicago: University of Chicago Press, 1992.

Purves, Alan C. *The Idea of Difficulty in Literature.* Albany: SUNY, 1991.

Rosenblatt, Louise M. *The Reader, the Text, the Poem: The Transactional Theory of the Literary Work.* Carbondale and Edwardsville: Southern Illinois UP, 1978.

Said, Edward W. *Beginnings: Intention and Method.* Baltimore: The Johns Hopkins UP, 1975.

Salvatori, Mariolina Rizzi. *Pedagogy: Disturbing History 1819–1929.* U of Pittsburgh P, 1996.

Salvatori, Mariolina Rizzi. "Towards a Hermeneutics of Difficulty." *Audits of Meaning.* Ed. Louise Z. Smith. Portsmouth, New Hampshire: Boynton/Cook Heineman, 1988.

Shulman, Lee S. "Disciplines of Inquiry in Education: A New Overview." *Complementary Methods for Research in Education.* Ed. Richard M. Jaeger. Washington, DC: American Educational Research Association, 1997. 3–30.

Steiner, George. *On Difficulty and Other Essays.* New York: Oxford UP, 1978.

Vygotsky, Lev. *Thought and Language.* Cambridge, Mass: MIT P, 1962.

Wiggins, Grant, and Jay McTighe. *Understanding by Design.* Alexandria, Virginia: Association for Supervision and Curriculum Development, 1998.

Inventing the Future

Lee S. Shulman
President, The Carnegie Foundation
for the Advancement of Teaching

F ROM 1968 TO 1975, I SPENT MUCH OF MY TIME as a faculty member helping to create a new medical school at Michigan State University. I became particularly interested in the clinical work of faculty members in medicine. Many of my professorial colleagues were physicians who cared for patients while also doing research and teaching. They read the medical literature voraciously to ensure that the clinical care they provided patients (and modeled for students) was state-of-the-art.

Many of them also conducted clinical research, both informally and formally. They carefully documented their diagnoses and treatment plans. They followed patients to track the course of treatments and responses. Periodically, they published sets of cases illustrating the efficacies of different interventions. At times, they moved from the systematic documentation of their clinical work to "clinical trials," more formal experimental studies in which experimental and control groups are compared over time. Thus, medical faculty not only engaged in scholarly healing; they contributed whenever possible, and in various ways, to a scholarship *of* healing.

I have often thought about my MD colleagues in recent years as I worked on the scholarship of teaching and learning. I have come to think of teaching as the clinical work of college and university faculty members. We serve our students by teaching them, just as medical faculty serve their patients through treating them. But while clinical research is a commonplace of clinical medicine, its equivalent remains rare in university teaching.

Even if promotion and salary were not intimately tied to the pursuit and publication of scholarship, most professors would feel an obligation to conduct some sorts of inquiry. Certainly, medical faculty accept a moral and pragmatic responsibility to monitor their clinical work and do whatever can be done to improve its impact. Isn't it odd that a parallel sense of responsibility has been so rare in college teaching? Our colleagues whose work in the scholarship of teaching fills this volume exemplify what I see as an emerging sense of this imperative. Their cases attest eloquently to the seriousness with which they accept this obligation.

Scholarly Fidelity
As I studied the cases in this volume, a single word kept forcing itself into my consciousness: *fidelity*. So much of the scholarship of teaching and learning is motivated by a spirit of faithfulness; such work expresses a deeply

professional commitment to the role of professor as teacher, mentor, steward, and public servant. There are four kinds of fidelity to consider:

- to the *integrity of the discipline* or field of study;
- to the *learning of students* one is committed to teach and to serve;
- to the *society, polity, community, and institution* within which one works; and
- to the teacher's own *identity and sense of self* as scholar, teacher, valued colleague, or friend.

The commitments listed here are not random. They remind us of the deeper meanings associated with the role of *professor* and *professional*. The primary meaning of "profess" is to profess one's faith, one's commitment, and one's life to service. A "professional" is someone who directs her intellectual and practical accomplishments to the service of her society and community. A member of a learned profession dedicates his understanding and skill to making complex judgments in the interests of his clients.

The cases in this volume illustrate each of these kinds of professional fidelity. They often overlap. The very same action by a teacher can reflect, for example, both commitment to the integrity of the discipline and to one's students. They occasionally conflict, as well. Thus, in order to pursue a goal consistent with the interests of the students, the teacher may have to challenge some expectations of the institution.

To teach, for instance, a scholar needs to transform a discipline as he knows it into a "school subject." The introductory course in American history is rarely organized as an historian understands and thinks about the field. It has been reframed to be more appropriate to novices. Similarly, a course in psychology typically follows a well-practiced organization and perspective. But does there come a point where the school subject has

drifted so far from the teacher's conception of the discipline that the integrity has been irreversibly compromised? And how does this sense of integrity interact with other commitments and "fidelities"?

Several of the cases in this volume are instructive in this regard. In the work of Mills Kelly in history, Donna Duffy in psychology, and Mona Phillips in sociology, we observe, in each case, a teacher-scholar who finds that the school subject lacks the defining characteristic of the discipline. For Kelly, the survey course bears little resemblance to the dynamic field of investigation and richness he knows as history. For Duffy, her course on abnormal and personality psychology rests on an older conception of the field rather than on the contemporary perspective she would prefer to take. For Phillips, the form of the course has drained it of both the intellectual zest and the emotional impact that the systematic study of their social world should offer to students. The challenge for these scholars is how to redesign their course to reflect more faithfully the discipline they have come to love and understand.

When Mills Kelly eschews the traditional Western Civilization survey course at Texas Tech University for a more thematic, focused, and methodologically sophisticated course, he is enacting his sense of the integrity of the discipline of history, which he feels is violated by the superficial survey. History, for Kelly (and many others), is not a superficial race through time, a high-speed journey "from Plato to NATO." It is problem-centered, not answer-anchored. It digs deeply into a period, unearthing contradictions, complications, and subtleties. These are features not encountered in the traditional survey. So he redesigns his course, drawing on the power of the new instructional technologies, to offer his students a chance to experience the depth and texture of historical reasoning and analysis. Will this work? Can students learn world history in this manner? How will they respond? What will they learn? What attitudes will they develop? Note that his concerns about fidelity to the discipline clearly cross over into questions reflecting his commitments and responsibilities to students.

Donna Duffy teaches one of the most popular courses in psychology, the study of abnormal psychology and personality. This course has traditionally focused on psychopathology, a topic that students typically find fascinating. Neuroses and psychoses, schizophrenia and character disorders, ink-blots and dream analysis—these are classic topics in the psychology of personality. But Donna, who teaches at Middlesex Community College, knows that the field of psychology has been undergoing a sea-change in how it treats these topics. A growing body of psychologists—Duffy among them—has helped to engineer a veritable paradigm shift in the field. Modern psychological theory has transferred much of its attention from deviant and abnormal behavior and its contextual determinants to an engagement with understanding the miracles of resilience, survival, and success against the odds. Donna not only believes that her students will learn more effectively from that perspective, she believes that her orientation is more faithful to the emerging changes in her discipline. And as reported in her case, she has been studying how the new course is learned and understood by her students. Her fidelity to the discipline and to students also entails a sense of responsibility to the institution as she works with colleagues to explore questions that are crucial to the success of community college students.

When Mona Phillips engages in the teaching of sociological theory, she is deeply troubled by her students' difficulties with understanding theory. She is even more concerned with her failure to help them experience the *joy* of curiosity and inquiry, the thrill of speculation, the excitement of systematic explanation and deep understanding. If they cannot experience the cognitive and emotional concomitants of sociological understanding, she has not fulfilled her obligations as a steward of her discipline; she has failed to profess her own understanding and her love of knowledge (philo-sofia). So Mona sets out to restore for her students the excitement she associates with learning sociology. Her efforts are motivated by a concern for the integrity of sociology, for the intellectual and emotional lives of her students, and also, I believe, her own values and identity as a scholar.

Dennis Jacobs' work reflects a different dynamic of commitments. As he tells us in his case study, his scholarship of teaching has its genesis in seeing the significant consequences of student failure. He recognized that those students who do not succeed in introductory chemistry courses are frequently unable to pursue long-held career goals, such as becoming physicians. He then asked how he might be able to teach the course more effectively and inventively in order to make it possible for those students to succeed. In shifting the burden of responsibility from one borne exclusively by the students, he asserted that a significant portion of the "failure" was one of teaching and not solely of learning. There began his efforts at course redesign and evaluation.

Dennis also ruefully reports a paradox. "Some colleagues find it ironic that as I move deeper into the scholarship of teaching, I'm actually doing less teaching, but I would claim it's important to have this time for analysis and reflection." To pursue the scholarship of teaching more vigorously, he has had to become a less active teacher. He wonders if this is a fundamental contradiction, an irony of sorts.

I would argue that, far from being a contradiction, Dennis' paradox stands as a deep truth. It is true of other clinical domains as well. My colleagues in medicine who both care for patients and conduct clinical research on the quality of care must arrange to care for fewer patients in order to conduct their research with integrity. In this sense, fidelity to students may conflict with fidelity to one's obligations to the institution or even to the integrity of the discipline. On the other hand, we may have a conflict between two aspects of fidelity to students: to those immediately in one's tutelage and to those more universally committed to the study of one's field. Here is where the obligations of scholarly teaching and the scholarship of teaching may conflict.

I believe I could argue in each of these cases that the scholarship of teaching reflects a convergence of disciplinary, moral, communal, and personal motives. If one is truly devoted to one's discipline, one is committed to transmitting and developing faithful conceptions and understandings of the discipline in students. Thus the integrity of the discipline leads to a sense of what is best for the students. The community expects no less from us; and we expect no less from ourselves.

How might these webs of commitments and responsibilities shape the work of higher education over the next five or ten years? How will they help us invent the future? In what follows, I will describe changes implied by the scholarship of teaching and learning at three levels—in our work as individual scholars, in the character of our institutions of higher education, and in the conception of the profession.

Changes in the Work of Individual Scholars: A Convergence of Methods

As the scholarship of teaching and learning moves to a more central place in the work of faculty, a number of changes will ensue or be implied. As illustrated by the cases in this volume, these changes include new models for teaching and learning, new relationships with colleagues, new career trajectories and options, and new conventions and "genres" for sharing work with colleagues. My focus here, however, given the focus of this volume on approaches to the scholarship of teaching and learning, is a change in our conception of scholarly methods.

In modern times, we regularly distinguish between two kinds of method: the methods we use in our research, on the one hand, and our methods of teaching, on the other. In the older traditions of the university, however, these two aspects of method converged (or were never separated). The methods of scholarship and the methods of teaching were identical; one's "methods" were those strategies used to marshal evidence in a systematic and persuasive manner for instructing one's students. Both pedagogical and scholarly arguments involved warrant (evidence) and explanation, in a persuasive rhetorical form. It is ironic that the two have not only drifted apart; they are seen as competitive.

When we think about the methods of research, we think of work unfolding over time. No one gets an idea and immediately begins to "do research." We recognize that research nearly always begins with general questions that need to be refined, with a stage of early design often leading to a formal proposal, and with preparatory or pilot work. The philosopher David Hawkins referred to the "preparation" period in scientific research, which can often take longer than the active empirical or experimental work itself.

We also recognize that research does not end with data collection. There ensues a long period of analysis, reconceptualization, writing and/or speaking, and dissemination of results. As Ernest Boyer observed in *Scholarship Reconsidered*, scholarship is incomplete until it is understood by others. Preparing your findings so they are understood and accepted by others is a serious challenge. Moreover, it is a powerful process for sharpening those findings. In a study of physicists, anthropologist Elinor Ochs found that when investigators were required to stop their research in order to prepare and present interim results, they engaged in powerful rethinking and synthesis. Having to present their work to colleagues was not a deflection of energy but an enhancement to the investigative process. In short, reflecting on one's investigations in order to present them to others engages the scholar in deeper thinking about her findings, and hence a deeper understanding of her own work.

Interestingly, we have not thought of teaching in this same way; there has not been a realization that good teaching is not simply *more* teaching, nor that the best teaching may require periods of reflection and analysis. This, of course, is the argument put forward by Dennis Jacobs and indeed, in various ways, by all of the case authors represented in this volume. I would vigorously affirm their conviction. Reflection and analysis are as essential for the scholarship of teaching as for any other kind of scholarly work. I believe that as the scholarship of teaching and learning takes hold, and as we generate a powerful body of work from the efforts of individual scholars, the distinction traditionally made between the methods of teaching and those of research will gradually disappear. Each will be understood as a variety of methodologically sophisticated, disciplined inquiry. Each demands activities of design, action, assessment, analysis, and reflection.

Institutional Transformations: Teaching Academies

I believe that in the long run advances in the scholarship of teaching cannot be sustained by the efforts of isolated scholars working alone or in loose networks. Institutions in which these scholars work must develop more formal structures that merge the institution's commitments to both teaching and inquiry.

These institutions can then serve as platforms for the work of scholars of teaching, as sanctuaries for their efforts, and as forums for their scholarly exchanges. Movement in this direction is indicated in many of the cases in this volume, which recount how the work of the individual scholar was supported by, or helped to foster, broader initiatives within the institution. In a previous paper entitled "Visions of the Possible," focused on institutional support for the scholarship of teaching and learning, I outlined several models through which local institutions can develop capacity for the scholarship of teaching by developing "teaching academies." That paper is available on the CD-ROM accompanying this volume, but I will describe two of its models here as well.

My first model—the teaching academy as interdisciplinary center—draws together faculty members whose scholarly interests include teaching and learning but who may not find a sufficient group of colleagues for this work within their own academic departments and professional schools; the idea behind this model is to overcome intellectual isolation by creating a new, multidisciplinary community of shared interests and work.

Think, in this regard, of women's studies centers, and how such centers have provided a kind of intellectual home for scholars from a variety of fields—history, economics, literature, and other areas—making possible important new work and the development of a new field. Historically, such centers made it possible to engage with important issues, to build knowledge, and to create new outlets for the work. The journal *Signs*, for instance, developed out of the Women's Studies Center at Stanford, and remains one of the primary scholarly journals in the field. At first these centers had a shaky sort of existence (publication in *Signs* was not held in high regard in its early days), but over time more stable, secure entities evolved. Stanford now houses the Institute for the Study of Women and Gender because the work done in these centers became more and more legitimate in the departmental and professional school homes from which scholars originally migrated to find more hospitable settings.

Or think of area studies and the centers for, say, African or Asian studies that began to emerge a couple of decades ago. Philanthropic foundations were extremely important in helping develop area studies. Here again we saw the phenomenon of building community across disciplines. In any given department you were likely to be the only Africanist. But, if you could develop an African studies center, you might gather together fifteen people on the campus, along with graduate students, and begin to find colleagues and to establish a kind of intellectual *gravitas*. You remained both historian (or geologist) and Africa scholar. Happily, universities and foundations found reasons jointly to support these efforts, which have in turn influenced the work and shape of many fields.

This kind of evolution is one of the things we would want for centers dedicated to the scholarship of teaching and learning, as well. In the best cases, scholars retain dual citizenship in both disciplinary department and center—and we would also hope for this for faculty affiliated with centers for the scholarship of teaching.

It should be said in reference to this first model that interdisciplinary structures entail both strengths and potential weaknesses. My colleague Larry Cuban recently completed a study of teaching and research at Stanford over the last 100 years—entitled *How Scholars Trumped Teachers*—and one of his themes is that at Stanford interdisciplinary entities were far more likely to innovate in teaching and curriculum than entities located in a single department. How does this happen? Many departments treat teaching the same way they treat research. That is, I wouldn't dream of telling my departmental colleague

what she should investigate in her research. Neither, in most departments, would I dream of telling her what she should teach. Most departments in most research universities support a conception of academic freedom in which all aspects of the faculty member's intellectual work is fully under her or his control. Curricula thus reflect the tastes of faculty members rather than a more superordinate conception of what and how students might best learn the field. But, as Larry Cuban shows, when you move to an interdisciplinary center, you leave behind some of these predispositions; making an active choice to join such a center, faculty are choosing to do something new. At Stanford an example would be the human biology curriculum, which cuts across several schools and many departments, and which allows new and different work both in the research that faculty conduct and in their teaching and curriculum development.

The handicap of such interdisciplinary programs is that the reward structure continues to go through the department. You can't get tenure in women's studies, or area studies, or human biology, but only in economics, or history, or biology. I'm not unhappy about that. Centers and institutes are intended to be more flexible and adaptive than their more conservative departmental godparents. But we must recognize that there is an essential tension between these structures, which would have to be dealt with if we took certain views of what teaching academies might look like.

My second model is the teaching academy organized around technology. My vision here is of a teaching academy whose reason for existence is connected to rapid developments in the use of technology in higher education. Technology is the 300-pound gorilla that no one can ignore, and this new element in all of our lives has had a healthily disruptive impact on our old habits.

For example, many faculty members are now asking serious questions about teaching and learning: How do we know these new technologies are effective in fostering student learning? What does student learning look like, and how do we know it when we see it? What's the difference between the kind of learning that occurs in traditional venues and the kind that occurs in technologically mediated settings?

The first advantage of this model of the teaching academy is that it builds on the fact that just about everybody agrees that teaching, learning, and technology pose serious research questions. Most universities have already committed significant resources to the uses of technology. And, since technology is not something you simply plug in, such research questions spawn a much larger set of inquiries about the curriculum, the design of instruction, and assessment, thereby encouraging a more general spirit of inquiry about teaching and learning.

There's a second advantage as well: To call something scholarship is to claim that it's public rather than private, that it's susceptible to peer review and criticism, and that it can be built upon by others. What technology has done in much of our pedagogy is to make the private public—through course Web sites, through the posting of syllabi online, through electronic resources such as the Crossroads Project developed by Randy Bass (a faculty member from Georgetown University, and a 1998 Carnegie Scholar) for the American Studies Association—not coincidentally, perhaps, an interdisciplinary field. On Randy's site you can see syllabi from American Studies courses around the country and also read annotations of these syllabi both by the people who created them and by others who bring relevant experience as reviewers. Similarly, the American Historical Association has established a Web site where peer reviewed course portfolios will be available. And at the Carnegie Foundation, as well, we are developing an online gallery of multimedia prototypes for documenting and displaying the scholarship of teaching and learning; examples from this site are available on the CD-ROM. My point is that through resources like these we have moved a good distance toward a public and exchangeable discourse about teaching and learning, which is a key ingredient in transforming conversations about teaching and learning to a scholarship of teaching and learning that occupies a central role in a discipline or interdiscipline, and on the campus.

There are many possible models of the teaching academy, certainly. The two here are meant to be illustrative, and to open up some of the issues entailed in forging such structures. I will end this section with what is both a hope and a prediction—that a wide variety of approaches to supporting the scholarship of teaching will evolve over the next decade. Indeed, the cases collected here make clear that institutions, programs, and departments must find their own ways to move in this direction. As demands for accountability become more commonplace, institutions must develop their capacities to ask hard questions about teaching and learning in order to explain their priorities, their expenditures, and their plans. This sort of institutional research can be pursued defensively, protecting the school's exposed flanks from attacks by skeptics. But accountability (I might call it institutional fidelity) can also serve as a powerful rationale for encouraging and supporting the work of faculty members whose research focuses on the instructional mission of the campus.

Changes in the Profession: The Future of the Doctorate

Efforts in the scholarship of teaching have led my colleagues and me at the Carnegie Foundation to conclude that both the doctorate and the culture of doctorate-employing institutions must change. There is a growing mismatch between the responsibilities that most college and university faculty members undertake on a daily basis, and the preparation they have received as they earned their field's highest degree. This observation prefigures the future for both the Carnegie Foundation and CASTL. While continuing our efforts at fostering a scholarship of teaching and learning for current faculty members, we are obliged to direct attention toward the programs that prepare future faculty members—doctoral preparation programs.

In urging such work, we join a long tradition of concern with doctoral preparation for faculty roles. In 1896, the University of Chicago's first president, William Rainey Harper, observed:

> It is an opportune moment to lay emphasis upon the work of teaching as distinguished from that of investigating. There is danger that the importance of teaching may be overlooked. The young doctor sometimes forgets that the institution in which he works is under obligation to furnish the best possible instruction to the students whom it has gathered within its walls.... If a man is unable to teach, he cannot rightly receive an appointment in the University. If, after having been appointed, he shows inability to teach, The University, in justice to its students, must without question find someone to take his place who is able to teach. (383–384)

Some thirty-four years later, a new president at Chicago, Robert Maynard Hutchins, would lay the responsibility for this problem at the feet of PhD programs. In his inaugural address, Hutchins urged the university to recognize that the primary function of the PhD program is to prepare college and university teachers, not to prepare investigators. Neither man truly believed that those who prepare individuals for the doctorate must necessarily choose one emphasis or the other, either investigation or pedagogy. However, each felt deeply that the role of doctor as teacher was already receiving but the shortest of shrift.

Carnegie's emergent work on the PhD shares this view, but our foundational claim is a different one: that a college professor is a member of a learned *profession*. A professional takes upon herself the obligation to serve others through exercise of the intellectual, practical, and prudential talents that her community has made available to her through education. Rather than make impossible choices between doctor as researcher and doctor as teacher, I argue that possessors of the doctoral degree assume the responsibility to serve as stewards of their discipline or profession. The doctor must take responsibility for the quality of the discoveries and inventions made in the field, the uses to which such knowledge is put, the critical review of the work of others who offer new ideas and proposals, and the instruction of the next generation of students and future scholars.

Where have these ideas come from? Carnegie's current work on education for the professions includes a study of education for the law. In doing this study, I have become acquainted with the concept of the lawyer as "an officer of the court." That is, when you complete your training as an attorney, pass the bar, and are admitted into the practice of law, you have two often-competing roles. You are to be a zealous advocate for the interests of your client, *and* you are to be an officer of the court who retains an obligation always to act in a manner that preserves and sustains the system of social justice.

An officer of the court must respect codes of privacy and confidentiality, be a zealot with respect to what counts as evidence, and understand that evidence must be available to all sides of a dispute. Questions of warrant and of evidence permeate every aspect of legal professional work. It follows that one cannot learn to be an officer of the court in an elective third-year course in legal ethics, though that's the way it often is done. It is a set of ideas and practices that must pervade the educational experience.

Similarly, physicians can be caught in a conflict between acting in the best interests of their own patients, or in the best interests of the society *writ large*. Physicians are often caught in a bind between prescribing an antibiotic a patient desperately wants but doesn't need, and recognizing that, in some incrementally infinitesimal way, every time an unnecessary antibiotic is prescribed we raise the likelihood that resistant strains of disease-causing organisms will develop. So the physician's professional obligation is to be a zealous healer of the client, but at the same time to be concerned about the public health, the commons; this is the parallel in medicine to being an officer of the court.

If we accept the notion that a PhD prepares professionals (whose profession is scholarship in the broadest sense), then it too entails this sense of being "an officer of the court." Wherever the scholar goes, whether to Spelman College or to the University of Pittsburgh, whether to Middlesex Community College or to Procter and Gamble, the PhD carries with it not only an entitlement to practice but a sense of the responsibilities and obligations of the role. The true professional must, if you will, be a steward of the discipline or domain in which she or he is now the recipient of the highest recognition of scholarship.

What does such stewardship imply for the form of doctoral preparation? It implies, for starters, that the scholar cannot be so narrowly prepared in the field as to have little sense of the terrain around her or his specialization. A faithful steward cannot be narrow. Moreover, stewardship entails a kind of work that is reflective, responsible, and communal. That is, a responsible steward constantly scrutinizes the quality of his or her work, subjects that work to the critical examination of others, and joins in the work of professional communities dedicated to performing the functions that best serve the greater society.

A true scholar is a well-prepared professional. She is not simply one who *does* the work; a scholar is someone who regularly and constantly steps back from the doing and reflects on what it *means*. That's why writing is so important for scholarship. Scholars are obligated to share their ideas through publication, presentation, and teaching because going public is the ultimate test of the quality of an idea. Because this process is so powerful, we institutionalize it by creating learning communities of scholars, whether they be research teams or faculties, which expect and reward various kinds of publication and "going public." Reflection is very difficult to practice in isolation.

The second aspect of scholar-as-steward is responsibility. When we take on the cloak of scholarship, we take on responsibility for seeing that the standards of evidence, of warrant, of argument are taken seriously and upheld in our own work and in the work of others; we take responsibility, in some sense, for the purity of the intellectual environment. We review each other's work, whether for publication or for promotion. In these roles, we are stewards of the discipline or domain.

Finally, a scholar is someone who is communal; she not only cannot but must not keep secrets. Scholarship entails a responsibility to "pass it on," to exchange what you have learned, what you have found, what you have invented, what you have created, with the other members of your community, assuming that they will do the same for you. This commitment is essential because the work of the community transcends the ability of any single scholar or teacher to do it. And so, the role of scholar, communicator, and teacher-scholar converge in this aspect of the obligation of the scholar.

Speaking as the president of Johns Hopkins University, the very model of the American research university, Daniel Coit Gilman (who would later be appointed first president of the Carnegie Institution of Washington, an organization dedicated to pure scientific research) noted, "The scholar does but half his duty who simply acquires knowledge. He must share his possessions with others. This is done, in the first place, by the instruction of pupils" (57). In Carnegie's work to study and improve preparation for the PhD, we will pursue a multifaceted vision of doctoral preparation, one aimed at fostering capability along a number of scholarly dimensions, including, of course, the stewardly functions of teaching and the scholarship of teaching. Indeed, the scholarship of teaching will play an important role in our work as we seek to work with pilot programs and faculty to explore and study innovations.

We will work with a small number of leading doctoral programs (and their associated disciplinary and scholarly societies) as they experiment with different ways of defining and operating doctoral programs. Some of these "experiments" are already ongoing as part of a Preparing Future Faculty initiative or a similar program. Some will also grow out of our current efforts in the Carnegie Academy for the Scholarship of Teaching and Learning (CASTL), which will by the end of this next year involve more than 100 Carnegie Scholars (including the eight represented in this volume) working with us to develop new models of the scholarship of teaching and learning in their disciplines.

The key to our efforts in the study of the doctorate will not only be experimentation per se. Our intent is to treat these experiments as further sites and occasions for the scholarship of teaching and learning through an on-going process of research and of convenings. Over a five-year period we will bring together those who are providing leadership in re-envisioning, reconceptualizing, redesigning, and experimenting with these variations so they can learn from each other more intensively. We will work with them to develop better ways to document, analyze, and exchange data on their programs and on the intellectual, technical, and moral development of their candidates. Learning to be a "doctor" is as suitable a focus for the scholarship of teaching and learning as learning to do chemistry or learning world history. The doctorate is the source of each new generation of college and university professionals. We must understand the pedagogical processes that nurture or corrupt their professional development.

Opening Lines, Closing Ranks

The cases presented in this volume are the efforts of individuals, nurtured by a national Carnegie program and by their local institutions. Both kinds of support are necessary. Serious scholarship depends on the creation of intellectual communities that transcend institutional boundaries and link together working scholars with shared interests and investigations. When that scholarship is directed at the teaching and learning that occur at a particular institution, its efforts must be supported locally as well. For such research, the institution plays multiple roles, as both research site and interested partner in the investigation.

In the opening lines of this essay I recalled my years as a medical educator, and the dual roles played by clinicians in medical schools who both cared for patients and engaged in research on the efficacy of care. I continued the exposition by suggesting that scholars of teaching hold analogous roles in colleges and universities; we engage in the clinical work of teaching our disciplines and we conduct research on the efficacy and character of that teaching. In medicine, we call those institutions that take seriously the dual responsibility of clinical care and clinical inquiry "teaching hospitals." They are credible sites for teaching the next generation of medical practitioners precisely because they take their work so seriously that they investigate their own practice constantly.

What shall we call those institutions of higher education that take both teaching and inquiry into teaching seriously? Shall we call them "teaching universities" to parallel the concept of teaching hospitals? That seems rather redundant. Perhaps we ought to call them the "new research universities." Unlike the old research universities, their scholarship and sense of responsibility is both external and internal, both expressive and reflexive. Those would be institutions to which we could entrust the responsibility for educating the next generation of university and college faculty in PhD programs. And in the case of institutions without graduate programs, they would be those we would turn to as places that support new and current faculty in their ongoing investigations of teaching and learning. We could then close ranks behind a conception of the new research university—an institution that takes its work so seriously that it makes that work the most important focus of its own investigations.

Let me put this vision a little differently: I believe that by 2005 there will be a fundamental recognition at colleges and universities in the United States that good teaching requires serious investigation into teaching and learning. I believe we will begin to see a fundamental reconception of our shared understanding of good teaching. Ultimately, investigative work into teaching and learning will not be an intriguing aside, or an add-on, but an essential facet of good teaching—built into the expected repertoire of scholarly practice. How will we identify this shift? Faculty members will increasingly ask important questions about teaching and learning and find ways to go about answering them. Campuses will develop means to support faculty effectively in this work through teaching academies, through direct financial support, and through changes in the reward structures governing tenure and promotion. Graduate programs will develop ways to introduce the scholarship of teaching into their training. The public may even begin to recognize and value the increased knowledge about student learning and attention to effective practice. It is a future worth inventing, and one that is powerfully prefigured by the work presented in this volume.

REFERENCES AND RESOURCES

Boyer, Ernest L. *Scholarship Reconsidered: Priorities of the Professoriate*. Princeton, New Jersey: Carnegie Foundation for the Advancement of Teaching, 1990.

Cuban, Larry. *How Scholars Trumped Teachers: Change Without Reform in University Curriculum, Teaching, and Research, 1890–1990*. New York, NY: Teachers College Press, 1999.

Gilman, Daniel Coit. "Utility of Universities." *University Problems in the United States*. New York: Century, 1898. 43–76.

Harper, William Rainey. "Sixteenth Quarterly Statement of the President." *University of Chicago Record* 1.28 (1896): 383–384.

Hawkins, David. "Learning the Unteachable." *Learning by Discovery: A Critical Appraisal*. Ed. Lee S. Shulman and Evan R. Keislar. Chicago: Rand-McNally, 1966. 5–8.

Ochs, Elinor, and S. Jacoby. "Down to the Wire: The Cultural Clock of Physicists and the Discourse of Consensus." *Language in Society* 26.4 (1997): 479–505.

BIOGRAPHICAL
NOTES

BIOGRAPHICAL INFORMATION ABOUT THE EIGHT FACULTY whose work is featured in this volume appears at the opening of their respective case studies. Additional contributors are as follows.

Pat Hutchings Editor and author

Pat Hutchings is a senior scholar with The Carnegie Foundation for the Advancement of Teaching, where she and Lee. S. Shulman co-direct the Carnegie Academy for the Scholarship of Teaching and Learning. She joined the Foundation in 1998 after nine years with the American Association for Higher Education. Pat has written widely on the investigation and documentation of teaching and learning. She holds a doctorate in English from the University of Iowa and was a member of the English Department at Alverno College from 1978–1987.

Lee S. Shulman Author

Lee S. Shulman is president of The Carnegie Foundation for the Advancement of Teaching, a position he assumed in 1997, and Charles E. Ducommun Professor of Education Emeritus at Stanford University. A native of Chicago, Lee received his PhD from the University of Chicago, and then moved to Michigan State University where he was professor of educational psychology and medical education and founding co-director of the Institute for Research on Teaching. He is a former president of the American Educational Research Association as well as past president of the National Academy of Education. His work on teaching and learning has shaped work in both K–12 and higher education.

Laurie Milford Copy editor and production manager

Laurie Milford directs a faculty development project at the University of Wyoming, funded by the Hewlett Foundation. Previously, she worked with Pat Hutchings to coordinate work for the Carnegie Academy for the Scholarship of Teaching and Learning, especially CASTL's initiatives with the scholarly and professional societies. Laurie has provided editorial services to academic publishers since 1993. She has a master's degree in English from the University of Wyoming.

A number of additional Carnegie staff members played important roles in the development of this volume. Gay Clyburn, director of communications and information, oversaw the production and design process and proofread. Marcia Babb, program director for the Carnegie Academy for the Scholarship of Teaching and Learning, assembled and organized materials for the accompanying CD-ROM. Toru Iiyoshi, technical director of Carnegie's Knowledge Media Laboratory, worked with Marcia to design and produce the CD-ROM.